Psychic Animals

PSYCHIC ANIMALS

An Investigation of their Secret Powers

by

DENNIS BARDENS

ROBERT HALE · LONDON

© *Dennis Bardens 1987*
First published in Great Britain 1987

Robert Hale Limited
Clerkenwell House
Clerkenwell Green
London EC1R 0HT

British Library Cataloguing in Publication Data

Bardens, Dennis
  Psychic animals: an investigation of
  their secret powers.
  1. Parapsychology and animals
  I. Title
  591   BF1045.A6

ISBN 0-7090-2922-5

Photoset in Ehrhardt by
Rowland Phototypesetting Limited,
Bury St Edmunds, Suffolk
Printed in Great Britain by
St Edmundsbury Press Limited
Bury St Edmunds, Suffolk
Bound by WBC Bookbinding Limited

Contents

Foreword by David Bellamy	7	
List of Illustrations	9	
Acknowledgements	11	
Introduction	13	
1 Animals: Their Sixth Sense	25	33
2 Dogs and ESP	37	
3 The Homing Instinct	56	
4 Dogs – Friends of Man	69	
5 A Flash of Strange Light	79	
6 The Inexplicable Cat	89	
7 Cats: Their Secret Wisdom	102	
8 Horse Sense	112	
9 Phantom Horses	122	
10 The Mysterious Dolphin	130	
11 Ape and Essence	141	
12 Animals as Gods – The Mystic Link	154	
13 Birds as Gods	163	
14 Animals and Magic	172	
15 The Psychic Jungle	177	
16 Non-Human Psyches	189	
Bibliography	195	
Index	197	

Errata
Pages 130 and 200: *for* Bob Holman *read*
Bob Holborn

Foreword

Like most botanists, zoologists and ecologists, I find that despite a lifetime's interest in natural history, I am still learning more and more about the wonderful world of plants and animals.

My knowledge and wonder was increased still further when I read the draft of this remarkably interesting and totally 'different' book on the mysterious powers displayed by animals of all kinds.

The author has presented in his own most interesting and readable style, the results of his research within the diverse fields of animal behaviour.

People are not only the most destructive of all living things, they are also the most arrogant concerning their special powers and place in evolution. Whether this book will help deflate that arrogance I can only guess. However, I feel quite sure that those who read it will find themselves observing animals, and perhaps themselves too, in an entirely new light.

David Bellamy

List of Illustrations

Between pages 96 and 97

1	The Gayer-Anderson cat
2	Greyfriars Bobby
3	Jack the baboon
4	The duck that saved a town
5	Heidi the dachshund
6–7	Guide dogs for the blind
8–9	Henrietta the Capuchin monkey
10	Queenie the alsatian
11	The Akita dog
12–13	Percy the dolphin
14	John Aspinall's tigers

Picture Credits

The following photographs have been reproduced by kind permission of: The British Museum: 1; Mary Evans Picture Library: 3; The Guide Dogs for the Blind Association: 6, 7; Leslie Lee: 12, 13; Metropolitan Police: 10; Rita Nannini: 8, 9; Willy Pragher: 4; The Press Association Ltd: 14; The Scottish Tourist Board: 2; Visnews: 11.

Acknowledgements

In a book as fact-crammed as this it is clearly impossible to list all who have been of help to me. Nevertheless, with the reservation that all who are not specifically mentioned have my gratitude and appreciation, I would like to express my particular thanks to the following:

To Professor Joan Willard, of the Albert Einstein College of Medicine of Yeshiva University, New York, for information on the Capuchin Monkey Training Project; Miss Eleanor O'Keefe of the Society for Psychical Research; the Guide Dogs for the Blind Fund; the Metropolitan Police; Bob Holman the deep sea diver for his invaluable insight into dolphin behaviour; Charles Sweeting of the British and Commonwealth Institute of New York; Miss Janet Grant; Miss Diane Schluger and Miss Christine Wiener.

I am also indebted to the editor of *Psychic News*, Tony Ortzen, and his staff for their cheerful and willing assistance.

My thanks are also due to Mr Rivers Scott of Scott Ferris Associates, for his patient advice and guidance and finally – and especially – to Dr David Bellamy, the distinguished naturalist and zoologist, for his kindness in reading the original manuscript and writing his introduction to it.

To all my numerous correspondents throughout the world, thanks for your help and co-operation.

Introduction

In 1983 frantic search parties were combing the rugged cliff tops, coves and coastline of Menorca, looking for a little boy of three who had disappeared while on a picnic with his parents on the cliffs near their home in Villacarlos. For thirty hours the parents of Oscar Simonet joined the search parties organized by the Mayor, Jose Tadeo. Frogmen probed creeks and inlets. Sadly, it was assumed that the boy had fallen into the sea, been drowned and washed out to sea.

When the Mayor, whose home was two miles away from the Simonets', got back to his house, his four-year-old Irish setter Harpo behaved totally out of character. Normally obedient, it simply would not let the Mayor settle down, and kept whining and running to the front door, scratching as though insisting on being let out.

Much puzzled, the Mayor followed as the dog led him to the spot at which the boy had disappeared, wagging its tail and making little barks all the while. At one point it stopped at a crevice hidden by undergrowth, which search parties had passed many times. Crashing his way through the thick entangled mass, Mayor Tadeo found Oscar lying semi-conscious; he had crawled into the undergrowth and fallen into a three-foot crevice, hitting his head upon the rock.

Everyone, not least the local veterinary surgeon, was puzzled and delighted. How, they asked, could a dog possibly have known where the boy was? The dog was two miles away when Oscar went missing. Although Irish setters are known for their high intelligence, this smacked more of clairvoyance or extra-sensory perception.

How did the dog know who or what the searchers were looking for? How did it lead them to the precise spot?

In 1980 a seagull saved a woman's life. The circumstances, corroborated from many reliable sources, are these:

Eighty-two-year-old Miss Rachel Flynn, of Cape Cod, New England, USA, was taking a walk on her own, as she loved to do amidst the gaunt and rugged scenery, when she fell over a thirty-foot cliff onto a lonely beach. Shocked and too badly hurt to move, she thought she would be left there until she died. As she lay trapped between large boulders, a seagull hovered over her. Seagulls look much alike to us, but Mrs Flynn thought that it *might* be one that she and her sister fed regularly at their home and which they had got to know so well that they called her Nancy. It seemed a long shot, but she remembers saying, 'For God's sake, Nancy, get help.'

The gull flew off to Rachel's home a mile away, where her sister June was working in the kitchen. June was irritated by the gull continually tapping the windowpane with its beak, flapping its wings frantically and, to quote her own words 'making more noise than a wild turkey'. She tried to shoo her away, but Nancy would not fly away or cease her noise. At last, after fifteen minutes June decided that, unlikely though it seemed, the bird was trying to tell her something.

The bird flew ahead, even stopping occasionally to see that she was being followed. She alighted at the cliff edge. June looked over the cliff and saw that her sister was trapped. She called the fire brigade, and Rachel, with a badly twisted knee and severe bruising, was taken to hospital.

June was in no doubt that the bird had saved her sister's life. 'It was simply incredible,' she told reporters, 'the way she came to the window and caused all that racket.'

How did that wild bird (it was *not* a pet) know somebody was in distress? How did it know the means to summon assistance?

Let us take another example of mysterious senses that animals possess.

In 1977 Kirsten Hicks, aged fifteen then, was due to leave Adelaide, Australia, with his parents on a long trip overseas. He asked his grandparents, a thousand miles away on Queensland's

Gold Coast, if they would look after his Persian cat, Howie. They cheerfully agreed but on his return had to tell the boy that his pet had vanished and all efforts to trace it had failed.

A year later the cat turned up at Kirsten Hicks' home. It was matted, filthy, footsore and bleeding. Yet it purred away happily on being reunited and with family care was soon restored to health.

The mystery of its amazing thousand-mile journey remains. Its twelve-month trek had taken it across rivers, deserts and vast tracks of wilderness and through rocky, rugged territory, largely uncharted (at least unknown to many). All of that area covered was totally unknown to it. How on earth did it know what route to take?

That animals possess strange and unexplained powers has been generally recognized for thousands of years, as I hope to show. That monuments have been erected, at various times and in different countries, to animals and birds is further confirmation of the respect, and sometimes awe, in which they have been held. (There are monuments to dogs, geese, dolphins and other animals of all descriptions.) Many commemorate acts of sacrifice and bravery, of disasters averted or lives saved by the intervention of an animal. But again, what could account for the rapport that exists between certain humans and animals that are otherwise fierce and powerful? Joy Adamson and her amazing rapport with the lion Elsa reminds us not only that 'wild' animals are seldom purposely cruel (as are humans), but that they can be gentle and loving to those they accept as friends. Joy Adamson, ironically enough, met her death at the hands of another human being, not from the dangerous beasts she moved amongst. In the 1960s the intrepid June Kay (Okavango) was proving the same point, keeping two lions as pets. The late and the last Emperor of Abyssinia (now Ethiopia), Haile Selassie, proved by his life a similar point, moving happily and fearlessly among the lions that roamed free in his palace at Addis Ababa.

The supposed 'psychic' propensities of animals have gained increased scientific attention since the turn of this century. Even before the Russian Revolution the Russian physiologist Bechterev was convinced that animals could be telepathic and could themselves be subject to mental influence from humans. The Soviet Union continued such research after 1917, while in the USA study of psi qualities in animals (telepathy, precognition and so on) caused the late Professor J. B. Rhine of Duke University to publish, in 1929, his investigations into the case of a supposedly telepathic horse.

In the course of writing two books on occult and strange subjects – *Ghosts and Hauntings* and *Mysterious Worlds* – I was struck with how often animals featured in the accounts either recorded in various archives or reaching me from informants. Reports of ghostly animals were quite frequent, examples of unusual rapport between humans and animals very numerous, and cases of seeming telepathy a constant occurrence. I decided, within the limitations of time and my own capacities, to make separate enquiries into this field, and this book is the result. It points the way, rather than providing dogmatic answers to very obscure problems. A lifetime spent in factual research and exposition is my main qualification for the task, although, as a member of the Society for Psychical Research, I have had the benefit of much advice and help and the use of their considerable archives covering over a century. The society, I should hasten to add, is a *scientific* body founded by scientists and is not committed to any corporate view.

I am not a zoologist, breeder or pet-owner, so cannot claim to be in telepathic communication or to have had as a pet a precognitive elephant. But one does not need to be a sheep to be a judge of mutton.

The late Professor J. Gaither Pratt, the distinguished para-psychologist who studied the problem of 'psychic' animals for decades, had no doubt that animals possess ESP (extra-sensory perception). He quoted one case in particular which is quite baffling. A twelve-year-old boy in Virginia found a homing pigeon which had a permanent aluminium band on its leg with the identifying number 167. The boy kept the pigeon as a pet. Later the boy was taken to a hospital that was seventy miles from his home. After being there for a few days he told the nurse, during a raging snowstorm, that a pigeon was at the window trying to get in. The nurse opened the window and in flew his pet, identifiable by the number 167 on the band. When his parents called to see him, they were astonished to find the pigeon there, for they had taken care of it at home.

On 20 April 1976 a very experienced diver, Keith Monery, of Bishop Otter College, Chichester, Sussex, found himself in difficulties off Penzance, Cornwall. An unexpected mischance had put him in real peril. His life-jacket had filled with water, and although he discarded his fifteen-pound-weight belt, he had difficulty in reaching the surface. He was rapidly nearing exhaustion in the rough seas and gave the distress signal, waving his clenched fist to and fro. A friend who saw the signal, Mrs Carswell, dived in immediately and swam to the rescue – but another friend was quicker off the mark. Beaky, a twelve-foot bottle-nosed dolphin, streaked past her 'like a rocket'. The friendly mammal (for the dolphin is not a fish) got underneath its human friend and kept pushing him, again and again, to the surface.

Beaky the dolphin knew that Mr Monery was in trouble, and seemed to care. Yet nobody has yet determined what makes dolphins like human company. History and folklore abound in stories of their intelligence, playfulness and love of people. There is a rapport of some kind, perhaps even some element of telepathy or mind-to-mind communication of the sort so often found in man's relationship with other animals.

The same rapport, often with mysterious undertones, is manifested between dogs and their owners. For instance, towards the end of 1970, Jean-Marie Valembois left Black, his two-year-old sheepdog, at his cousin's home in Béthune, north-east France. Attached though he was to his pet, his job as a building worker did not allow him to take his dog along with him; it was his habit to go where the work was, which meant that he could not always secure board and lodging near to the building site, and, even if he did succeed in this, plenty of hotels and *pensions* would not admit pets. His new job was taking him to Châteaurenard, near Avignon. He assured his cousin that Black would soon become accustomed to, and accept, his new master, and left Black with him.

Jean-Marie reckoned, however, without the devotion of dogs

or their secret sources of perception, for one day a workmate said to him: 'There's a strange dog running around near the building site. It's pathetic to see him – sniffing and whining, looking frantically this way and that, running, running, looking, looking . . .'

Jean-Marie had a hunch that it might be his dog, even though he could not imagine how Black could possibly have made his way to a place he had never been taken to before, 500 miles from his home. He went looking for the stray, which leapt at him with such joy that he was almost knocked over.

Animal behaviour experts, and psychic researchers, have long been puzzled by this sort of thing, this unidentified propensity which some animals possess of tirelessly and unerringly seeking out their masters over vast distances and in strange territory. Two decades of research, including the investigations of Dr J. B. Rhine, the American parapsychologist, have failed to solve the mystery.

The link between dogs and men is *not* based solely on a dog's dependence on his master for food, shelter and companionship. A high degree of intelligence and altruism is often shown in quite different circumstances.

To take another example: In Malmo, Sweden, in May 1977 Leif Rongemo left his two-year-old daughter and his pet Alsatian, Roy, in the living-room of his flat while he went into the kitchen.

Returning a few minutes later, Mr Rongemo was horrified to find the casement window open and both his daughter, Anneli, and his dog missing. He looked out of the window into the street thirty-six feet below. He could see nothing unusual until, glancing to the left he saw his daughter, on all fours, crawling along a narrow ledge that went round the building, while behind her, whining and obviously distressed, was the Alsatian. Both were beyond arm's reach. If he made any noise to startle either of them, both could fall to their death. There was not enough width for either child or dog to perform a turn and come back to the window that way. If he, too, went onto the ledge, all three would almost certainly die. Quick as lightning, he arranged with his wife to call the fire brigade and, pending their arrival, rushed downstairs with a blanket which he and a neighbour held underneath the child.

Mrs Rongemo stood at the window, watching as the distance between herself and the child lengthened, holding her breath, praying for a miracle.

The miracle happened in a most unexpected way. Suddenly, Roy the Alsatian pushed forward and with a quick, deft movement seized the child's nappy in his jaws. Then, to the amazement of spectators below, he shuffled backwards, inch by inch, towards the window. The agonizing journey took three minutes. Mrs Rongemo at last grabbed the child while Roy jumped into the room, wagging his tail frantically.

Nobody stands any chance of convincing the Rongemo family that dogs cannot think. Indeed, the incident left them rather ashamed, for they had been on the point of selling Roy, because he seemed too big and rough to keep with a tiny child around. It goes without saying that Roy is still one of the family.

If dogs are often known to save the lives of their owners, cats, less demonstrative, seemingly more aloof, have their record of devotion and heroism too. In April 1970 a whole family was saved by a cat. Mr Michael Lousada and his two children were asleep in their home in Woburn Sands, Buckinghamshire, when lethal fumes leaked from a gas-fuelled heating boiler. The cat mewed and scratched persistently until the family awakened and were alerted to the danger. Enfeebled by the gas and very near to coma, Mr Lousada was just able to help his children out of the house, and the three recovered in hospital.

The survival instinct is very strong in animals. The cat has a keen sense of smell, and its first inclination, one would suppose, would be to get itself into fresher air, away from the noxious fumes. Instead, the cat's first action was to awaken its owners.

In the same year a case was reported where a cat raced through the flames to alert the owners when a house caught fire, and only then, when it was plain that its owners were leaving the building, went through the flames again, with many a backward look to assure itself that its owners were following.

I have mentioned these few cases, chosen at random from a

considerable number, in order to establish one point at the outset: certainly pets can love their owners, and owners can love their pets, but I am convinced that this mutual affection is not so simple as we are inclined to assume. The mysterious rapport, the extent to which animals so often live for, and not merely with, their owners, and the manner in which they are able to detect the thoughts, or anticipate the actions, of human beings, suggest that some form of telepathy may be at work.

Although biologists, zoologists, animal-behaviour experts and others have accumulated a wealth of information about the millions of species of animals, birds, fishes and insects on the earth, in the air and in the sea, there is still a tremendous amount that we do not know about their ways of living; even less are we informed as to their individual consciousness, or the workings of their individualities. We just do not know what they feel, or what they think. Even with species which have no brain, there is often a 'built-in' intelligence of a kind making possible adaptation to environment, defence against enemies, finding a mate, raising their young and getting their food. Fabre, the great French naturalist, stood in absolute awe of the complex and elaborately organized life of the bees. Professor William McDougall, whose *Outline of Psychology* is an acknowledged classic in its field and who pleaded half a century ago for psychical research to be brought within the orbit of university studies, confessed himself 'staggered' at the behaviour of a worm which, in a test he devised, solved a complicated problem with the intelligence of a human being.

But should we be surprised? Why should not animals have mental, perceptual or even psychic capacities which human beings do not possess? Why should they not possess psychic abilities in common with human beings?

In the physical field, human beings are inferior to other living creatures in many respects. If I possessed a jumping power comparable with that of the flea, which generates enough energy inside itself to jump 130 times its own height, I would be able to jump to a height of nearly 700 feet – nearly four times the height of Nelson's Column in Trafalgar Square. In so many ways we are inferior to other animals. We can't run as fast as the cheetah, or live to nearly 200 years, as some tortoises have been known to do. The Alsatian dog's sense of smell is a million times as acute as that of a man. Although human beings are driven by the sexual urge as much as most living creatures, the glandular signals emitted as a sex attraction, which are usually concealed by scent, hardly compare with the sex signals of the female moth, which can be detected by the male at a distance of seven miles. A male chimp has an infinitely stronger pull than a man of similar build. No man can swim as fast as the Gentoo penguin. We can't fly. And we can't walk upside down on the ceiling, like a spider or a fly. We do not have the echo-sounding and radar-style devices of the bat, by which it avoids obstacles and, although blind, seeks and captures its prey.

Outclassed as we are in so many physical capacities, it need not, therefore, surprise us if in matters pertaining to the psyche we are also surpassed. I am personally convinced that this is so. So many species have existed far longer than man, evolving in the process strange abilities which impress but puzzle us.

This is my own exploration of extra-sensory perception in animals and other living things. I am concerned with such phenomena as clairvoyance and precognition (the animal's ability to anticipate natural disasters such as earthquakes, and even man-made accidents), with cases of unusual rapport with humans, of animal reactions to ghostly and psychic phenomena. There is, too, the mystery of 'psi-training'.

There *is*, I am convinced, a mystical element in the close attachment between animals and humans. There is a case on record of a snake defending its master from attack, and the snake, as we all know, is thought of as the embodiment of menace. I have been told of one case where a monkey died of grief, willing its own death by refusing to eat. It was the much-loved pet and companion of a remote district officer in the days of the British Raj in India. In those days the uniforms worn on official duty were elaborate. One day the officer was called away on urgent business and, being kept away longer than usual, the monkey seems to have presumed its master's death. He donned his master's hat, took his sword and slept with them in his master's bed. When the officer returned, he found the monkey in his bed, starved to death.

There is in Edinburgh a monument to Bobby, a Skye terrier which loved his master (an impoverished shepherd known locally as 'Auld Jock') so much that, on his death, he stayed at his grave for fourteen years, until he himself died.

The citizens of Freiburg in Germany raised a monument to a duck which saved thousands of lives during World War II by warning the inhabitants of an impending air raid. No official warning was given of a heavy and sustained raid that claimed thousands of victims, but many took to the shelters as the duck took to the streets and disturbed them all with its frantic quacking.

In preparing this work *Psychic Animals*, I am well aware that their mental processes, and even more their psyches, *are* secret. We do not know *why* some animals will refuse to go into a building reputed to be haunted, or behave in strange ways when passing some haunted spot (sometimes refusing to pass it). There is also the fact that 'ghosts' and phantasms, including those seen many times in the same place by quite different people, are not merely of people but frequently of animals.

A huge proportion of the world's population believes that something of *human* personality or identity survives. The belief is inherent in many religions, Christianity included. We may well ask – man not being the only useful or worthy creature – why survival or immortality should be the prerogative of man alone. Many people, including a prominent High Anglican churchman, have said decisively that it is not.

It is not easy to imagine how the complicated balance of ecology, the interdependence of all living things, could be duplicated in a non-physical existence; stories of animal ghosts suggest that, if ghosts in general are considered proof of the survival of personality after death, the same may be held true of animals. I have heard of a cat which, on taking up its position in a chair once used by its dead predecessor, would arch its back, spit, open its claws and behave as if scaring off an invisible enemy. The files of both the British and the American Societies for Psychical Research include many such cases.

According to the Roman historian Plutarch, the traditional laws and precepts of Triptolemus, in Greek mythology the alleged inventor of the plough, included the injunction to 'honour your parents; worship the gods; hurt not animals'. Certainly in the ancient world the mystical qualities of animals were fully recognized. In the Egyptian and other religions animals were worshipped as gods, while some gods were half animal and half human. Ethiopia – Abyssinia as it was then – was once ruled by a dog-king, the animal being actually clothed in a gown and wearing a gold crown. His edicts and responses were deemed to be indicated by his barks and the tapping of his paws, interpreted by his retinue of priests.

On the subject of the unusual affinity that exists between human beings and some animals, and the extraordinary lengths to which animals will go to demonstrate their loyalty and love, the French scientist Charles Graven asks, 'How are such affinities between man and animal formed? What other theory, besides telepathy, could explain such phenomena?'

I shall later on have something to say about telepathy, which undoubtedly does play a part in communication between humans and animals and which is an ingredient of the rapport that exists between them. Followers of Buddhism and similar religions see in such relationships a reflection of the principles of reincarnation. Animals have been human in previous lives, and human beings have been animals.

It is still the case that the majority of humanity regard animals as creatures merely to be exploited for food, clothing or the pleasures of the hunt or, at best, confined in little prisons called zoos or circuses. Others see them simply as part of a backcloth, part of nature's scheme of things. But those who are in contact with animals for any length of time, and who are able to observe them constantly and at close quarters, know how much animals do and know which cannot be explained. They live in a mysterious and secret world of their own, and in their relationships with us we get evidence of behaviour and attributes comparable with what we call extra-sensory perception.

Which reminds me that for clarity's sake I propose to use 'extra-sensory perception' (ESP) as an inclusive term covering a wide range of psychic phenomena which can also, of course, be mentioned separately. Telepathy means mind-to-mind communication or, in the case of creatures which appear to have no brain, communication by some method other than the use of sense organs. Psychokinesis is the movement of objects by mental energy. By 'ghosts' I mean hallucinations of sight and sound which have a seeming reality – or even the mere *feeling* of menace where a presence is merely sensed. Precognition is foreknowledge.

Even where human beings are involved, such phenomena are even now the object of much scientific enquiry, little of which has proved conclusive. One must, therefore, turn quite often to theory and hypothesis in seeking an explanation of the phenomena which I describe.

In short, this is an exploration of the secret world of animals, the part played by ESP in the animal world.

1
Animals:
Their Sixth Sense

In October 1976 a group of seismologists, geologists and biologists gathered at the Centre for Earthquake Research at Menlo Park in California to discuss the subject of abnormal animal behaviour before earthquakes. Thirty-five experts produced a formidable body of evidence to show that all manner of animals (and, indeed, birds and insects) show by behaviour that is out-of-character that they can sense impending disaster.

The conference noted that living creatures went haywire long before humans were alerted to the danger. Dogs have run berserk. Cats have left their homes and taken to the woods. Chickens have suddenly flown into the trees. Snakes have come slithering out of their dens in the middle of winter. Rabbits, as well as rats, have entered houses, deer in the forests have jumped up and down, and fish have been seen leaping out of the water.

The real initiative, however, in the study of animal behaviour during natural disasters lies with the Chinese. They have long maintained that a careful study of the behaviour of animals just before an earthquake may provide the rudiments of a forewarning system; such studies have, in fact, enabled them to forecast eleven earthquakes in the last five years. Thousands of Chinese volunteers have been asked to look for anything unusual and, on the basis of past observations, the sum total of their observations may well give forewarning of future disasters. As the Chinese radio network put it in 1976: 'The Tibetan yak lay sprawling on the ground. The panda was holding his head screaming, and the swan got up from the water and lay down on the ground.' The uninterrupted barking of dogs has been found to be another warning of an earthquake.

The report by the United States Geological Survey for 1976 shows that year to have been the worst in modern times for earthquakes, which claimed a total death toll of 700,000 lives in China, Guatemala, Italy, the Philippines and Turkey. Had it been possible to predict where and when they would erupt, people could have been evacuated and thousands of lives saved.

The Chinese are habitually secretive about most things, but the Americans are making no secret of their intention to investigate the question of animals' foreknowledge of earthquakes and, as a result, even use them as a sort of 'barometer' or pre-empted seismograph. Thus, in one experiment aimed at sensing the coming of earthquakes, a few miles north-east of Los Angeles in the Californian desert near the 'Palmdale Bulge', a colony of mice have been placed in seven artificial burrows, and twenty kangaroo rats in cages above the ground. Their behaviour is monitored by electronic devices. The site was chosen because the 'bulge' was caused by the earth raising itself in an area where earthquakes have occurred, and experts believe it may presage a major shock. The rodents, it is hoped, will give warning by their behaviour in advance of the seismograph.

It was the study of animal behaviour which enabled the Chinese to predict with accuracy the earthquake in the Lianong Province in 1975 but no such warning could have been issued about the major earthquake which devastated the city of Tang-shan, a hundred miles to the east of Peking, on Wednesday 28 July 1976. Although the casualties in Peking itself were lighter than they might have been, hundreds of thousands died in the stricken zone.

On that occasion a golden retriever named Lisa gave officials of the British Embassy warning of the massive earthquake. She awakened the second secretary, Richard Margolis and his French-born wife, who were looking after her for her owners, Mr and Mrs John Boyd. The dog's incessant barking convinced them that something was going to happen and they aroused the other members of the embassy staff, who quickly fled the building. That 'quake was potentially 11,000 times as destructive as the atomic bomb which wiped out the city of Hiroshima in World War II.

For some time now, the Soviet Union has also been exploring the possibility of using the study of animal behaviour as the basis for an early warning system of natural disasters, and the Geophysical Institute in Moscow is engaged on a massive research programme. It had been noted that for several weeks before the Tashkent earthquake the animals were restless, and that an hour before the earthquake struck they would not go indoors. Dogs set up a howling or barked long and furiously. A local schoolteacher noted that even the ants seemed in a hurry to get away, leaving their anthills and scurrying off in search of another home.

The earthquake in the Udine region of northern Italy, near the Yugoslav border, which caused severe damage and loss of life on the night of 6 May 1976, was also heralded by the concerted barking of dogs. Ninda Steccoti, a sixty-one-year-old survivor, told Reuter's correspondent Patrick Meney that the animals of the town seemed to sense the disaster beforehand, and that her own dogs began barking madly. David Willey, the BBC's correspondent on the spot, telephoned a businessman in the city of Treviso, to the south of the disaster area, who described in quaint but graphic terms what had happened: 'Everyone ran out of the houses and the dogs were complaining and shouting all around.' But as we know, a good many dogs 'complained and shouted' long before the earthquake struck.

Before the Agadir earthquake in Morocco in 1960 stray animals, including dogs, were seen streaming away from the port before the shock that killed 15,000 people. A similar phenomenon was observed three years later, before the earthquake which reduced the city of Skopje, Yugoslavia, to rubble. Most animals seemed to have left before the 'quake. The Russians observed, too, that animals began to abandon Tashkent before the 1966 earthquake.

The Californian earthquake of 1979 was, according to the *Daily Telegraph*, also marked by strange and erratic behaviour of animals beforehand:

Their behaviour, observed by many full time keepers, supports the theory that animals are specially sensitive to seismic activity. Latest observations were made at the safari park in San Mateo county, three miles south of San Francisco and four miles from the notorious 'San Andreas earthquake fault line.' Mary O'Herron, a park official, said that 'on the evening before the llamas would not eat. That's unusual. They were running around wildly all the night.' A cougar had been 'restless'. A 'normally very nice' baby tiger curled up in a corner all day, refusing all friendly advances. An elephant refused to have his toenail trimmed – normally the elephant is very gentle. When she was returned to the barn she trumpeted and attacked the door.

That 'quake was the strongest to hit California for many years.

It is strange that this special sensitivity of animals should only recently have led to serious research into the subject, since the phenomenon of foreknowledge in animals has been noted for centuries. A Captain Fitzroy, in describing an earthquake at Galcahuasco on 20 February 1855, said that all the dogs left the town before the shock that brought the buildings crashing down. Similar behaviour by dogs was noted by observers in the earthquakes at Callao, Peru, in 1745; at Owens Valley, USA, on 26 March 1872, in Assam on 12 June 1897 and in Mexico on 15 April 1907.

Dr Ute Pleimes of the University of Geissen in Germany mentions a volcanic eruption on the French island of Martinique in the West Indies in 1902 as a classic case where the warnings of animals could have been heeded. On a seemingly calm day the animals of the island fled their homes in panic and made for the beaches before a volcanic explosion completely destroyed the city of St-Pierre, killing over 30,000 people. Many of the animals, even those who could not swim, plunged headlong into the sea. The islanders were convinced of coming disaster, but their fears were ridiculed at the local observatory.

Even if the capacity of dogs to foretell natural disasters such as earthquakes and floods should prove, subsequently, to have a natural explanation, it would still make sense to heed them, for experience has shown that they know better than human beings, even when humans are backed with elaborate and expensive instrumentation. So the Chinese are not so bizarre as some might think in their decision to observe animal behaviour closely as a safeguard against the sort of disaster which struck in 1976.

Are dogs capable of telepathy – mind-to-mind communication?

The short answer is: yes, they are. The facts are hardly arguable. A question put by a chemist in the Journal of the Society for Psychical Research in July 1950 was out-dated even then and is even more academic a quarter of a century later. He said then:

> The interaction of *psi* fields belonging to members of different groups is a further question . . . For instance, is the training of a dog by his master entirely dependent upon the 'normal' senses of both, or is there a contact directly between the *psi* fields of the two? Considering the limited intelligence of the dog, and the fact that in any *psi* interaction it is ideas and not specific symbols which are transmitted, it seems to me very likely that in the extremely well-attuned dog-and-shepherd pairs we have a transmission of the shepherd's intention to the mind of the dog . . .

Most dog owners, and a considerable number of dog trainers, have felt or expressed something of the kind. No doubt humans are given to minute involuntary movements of which they are unaware but which animals are quick to perceive, but there is ample evidence that dogs can actually read the minds of human beings, can sometimes know their thoughts. Sometimes they take appropriate action before those thoughts are even formulated!

In his presidential address to the Society for Psychical Research in 1962, Dr Gilbert Murray asked: 'Is there not some telepathy, some shared sensitivity at work – not very different from that which a dog feels when he shares the trouble or anxiety of his master?' A zoologist, Dr Maurice Burton, once conducted a simple experiment in telepathy with his boxer, Jason. He waited till Jason was asleep in an armchair, then he asked his daughter, who was in another room, to call the dog silently at a certain time. At the precise time they had arranged, the dog, which had been sleeping, awoke, jumped straight off the chair and went to his daughter. No sound had been made.

Foremost in research into animal behaviour (in particular, their more mysterious capacities) were the Russian scientist V. L. Durov and the famous physiologist V. M. Bechterev. Durov, who was an expert trainer of animals, devised a means by which he could give orders to dogs by telepathic means, making no sound of any kind by any means, and giving no sign. He would vividly imagine, in his mind, what he wanted the dog to do – to come to him, to jump over a chair, to sit, to bark, and in the majority of cases his dogs complied at the precise time in the exact way.

Durov occasionally noted that some unexplained time-factor was involved, the dog fulfilling not the task it was required to do but the task which came into the trainer's mind before he changed it. Further, when the unspoken command triggered some emotional response, that response would be repeated when it was not required that it should be – you could call it a 'sorcerer's apprentice' response in the sense that the experimenter could not easily stop what he had started, even though his initial command was obeyed. As an example of this type of response, the dog was told to bark violently at a stuffed animal.

Dr Bechterev, amongst other scientists, confirmed Durov's conclusions that some kind of 'sixth sense' was operating. He noted that the dogs fulfilled Durov's orders even in Durov's absence, thereby excluding any suggestion that the dogs might be responding to signals, however unwitting, made by him.

Dr Durov's laboratory in Moscow, which was state-supported, concentrated to a considerable degree on this question of telepathy and telepathic communication with animals. He did not work alone but in collaboration with a number of other scientists, and even in the first few months of the laboratory's existence 1,278 telepathic experiments with dogs were carried out, of which 696 were successful and 582 failures. A scientific evaluation along strict statistical lines, under the supervision of Professor L. K. Lakhtin, ruled out any possibility of these results being attributable to chance.

The inference was obvious: some ESP factor must be at work. It was mathematically preposterous to suppose that dogs could, in more than half of the unspoken commands, have responded correctly merely by chance. It would be tantamount to a human being backing every second number correctly on a roulette wheel, or getting half the draws right on a football-pool coupon. The odds against this would be billions to one.

By the time of his death in 1934, Durov had conducted no fewer than 10,000 such trials. One of his collaborators, B. B. Kazhinsky, introduced a new feature into the experimental pattern, to see if electro-magnetic radiation from the brain could be the answer. Durov was 'screened' in a box, and it was observed that, when his commands came from within the closed box, the response was less precise than when the door of the box was open. Years later, Professor Leonid Vasiliev, an associate of Bechterev, upon whose shoulders the primary responsibility for research into the nature of telepathy fell, proved by his own experiments that telepathic messages could be conveyed even in circumstances of the most stringent electro-magnetic shielding. Therefore he had reluctantly to admit (after endless research) in a paper, *The Transmission of Mental Images*, that the assumption that telepathy was based upon electro-magnetic radiation was unjustified.

Vasiliev, going upon his own experiments and those of his colleagues, favoured the view that telepathy is an atavistic instinct. As between humans, it may be a hang-over from the days when man had no language and developed, over millions of years, a means of communication without it. The same would hold true for other animals. In primitive conditions, life could depend upon it. Animals, not having developed a language in the sense that we mean, although they have many means of communication that include actual sound, are probably, he concluded, telepathic. He knew for a certainty that dogs are, both from watching Durov's experiments and from conducting his own.

Mrs Renée Haynes, an author and psychical researcher who is a well-known member of the Society for Psychical Research, once related a seeming case of telepathy in her own dog, which had had an operation for the removal of a tumour. 'The night before I was to collect her from the vet,' she recalled, 'I dreamt she had suddenly collapsed. The next day the vet phoned to say that the dog had had an unexpected haemorrhage and died in the night.'

An eerie example of telepathy and 'astral projection' combined, in the case of a pet dog, was reported in the *Daily News* in the 1920s.

> My wife had gone into town to shop, taking with her Bill, the bull-mastiff. Because of a cold, our small son Christopher, aged five, had remained at home with me. We sat by the fire in the all-but-dark, listening-in. The time must have been five-twenty; for the Children's Hour had begun about five minutes before. Without warning, in the midst of an uncle's delectable nonsense, Christopher gave a queer, low cry. I looked at him. In horror, I saw that his eyes were gleaming like a beast's, changing from green to red, and from red to green. The low cry was repeated; it was like a husky snarl, canine or vulpine – assuredly not human.
>
> I sprang forward and caught the boy to me. He was shivering. His face was like death. Slowly, the snarling died; the eyes lost their horrible gleaming. He said, sobbing, 'They're killing my Bill. He's dead, my poor Bill.'
>
> Shortly afterwards, my wife arrived in a taxi, very much shaken. An Alsatian dog had gone mad in the High Street. Chased by an excited crowd, it had leapt at my wife, and knocked her down. But for Bill, it would have bitten her. Bill had flung himself at the Alsatian's throat; the two dogs had fought; in the midst of their fighting, the vet had shot them both. That was at five-twenty.
>
> There is no explanation. Obvious theories suggest themselves. The sole, sure facts are that Christopher idolised Bill, and that the boy was as if possessed, at the moment of the dog's death.

Here is a phenomenon which cannot be fitted into any fixed category, since it seems to have in it an element of possession, telepathy and perhaps even haunting. The element of telepathy, of which there seems little or no doubt, lies in the fact that the boy was acutely aware that something was wrong, at the time his dog was dying.

Despite Professor Vasiliev's rejection of his original premise that telepathy must be based somewhere on electro-magnetic radiation, two Canadian scientists, reported in the *New Scientist* of 30 January 1975, believe that animals may use telepathy, communicating by a kind of microwave radio. J. Bigu del Bianco and Cesar Romero-Sierra, of the Anatomy Department of Queens University, Ontario, working on a National Research Council of Canada grant, investigated the microwave emissions (relatively weak electro-magnetic radiations, not unlike those used in radar and microwave ovens) from a man and a rabbit. Measurements were taken of the signals from the abdomen of a man, from a man's hand and a rabbit's head. Signals were detected in all cases and, in the case of the rabbit, signals of different strengths corresponded in intensity to different levels of stress. This brings to my mind the particularly heartless experiment in which Russian scientists took into a submarine the litter of a young rabbit, which was left ashore. The mother rabbit was linked up to an electronic detector by means of antennae, and then, one by one, her young were killed within the submarine. Every time one of the baby rabbits was killed, the mother rabbit reacted, at the very instant.

The Russian experiment was merely one of a whole complex network of research into the phenomenon of telepathy, the idea behind it being that if its precise working could be ascertained, it could then be applied for defensive and offensive purposes. The rabbit experiment proved that a means of communication other than sounds exists between them, just as the experiments of del Bianco and Romero-Sierra indicate that living creatures, men as well as animals, emit rays which are not purely mental but which may be related to telepathy and other such mysteries. Clearly, if such means of communication exist (and even scientists nowadays do not dispute the existence of telepathy), they may operate not merely between men and men, and between animals and animals, *but between man and animals*. Animals are as much 'in' on ESP as we are, and probably to a far greater extent, so many of the species being so much older in evolution than man and having had far more time to develop propensities.

Among the ESP powers of animals we have yet to establish is the high probability that they can see not only the human aura but the auras of their own and other species.

There was a time when the aura was considered a fanciful idea. Semian Kirlian, of Krasnodar, in the Soviet Union, is an electrical technician who, like most of his kind, enjoys tinkering about in his workshop. A few years ago, quite by accident, he discovered that the aura, hitherto believed to be bands of coloured light radiating from and surrounding human beings, animals and plants, did exist. Baron von Reichenbach in the nineteenth century had already claimed to have discovered such radiations; Kirlian, however, demonstrated and proved them.

Kirlian discovered one day that if you touch with your fingers light-sensitive paper within the force-field of high-frequency electrical currents, the paper will show lines and dots. There was *something* emanating from the finger. What could it be? He developed a new apparatus and new photographic technique. With his wife Valentina, a journalist, he developed fourteen new inventions, subsequently much simplified. By means of a high-frequency apparatus they could photograph the 'transmissions' from living things and creatures. A light-sensitive paper or film is placed over the object – it could be anything, a coin, a leaf from a tree or plant, a finger – and the high-frequency current is switched on. The photo is ready.

Some Kirlian photographs are amazing in their complexity and beauty – some for all the world like firework displays. The microscope, allied to the technique, reveals an incredible range of vivid colours which, in the case of humans and animals, change according to the mood.

Whether we are aware of it or not, therefore, communication between humans, between animals and between animals and humans is often operating not only while they are in proximity but at a distance.

In *Bandoola*, a fine book about elephant management in Burma, J. H. Williams relates how, by concentrating his will-power, he was able to make his Alsatian, Molly Mia, come to him from a considerable distance.

A story of telepathy with a psycho-kinetic element was told to me by Mrs Anne Excell, a bookseller in Brighton. Her family possessed a crossbred Labrador which had been born with deformed hip joints. Although this deformity was not visible, it showed clearly on X-ray plates and explained why, on occasions, Jack, as he was called, refused to move. The vet said that, although his joints were in a bad state, the dog would probably develop strong muscles and learn to live with his condition. All went well for five years, but suddenly Jack could neither stand nor walk. His grieving owners took him to a vet, who felt nothing could be done. A visit to London Veterinary College for another opinion merely confirmed the first. So they took him back to the first vet, who suggested the dog be left with him for a couple of days, although it seemed fairly certain that he would have to be destroyed. I give the sequel in Mrs Excell's own words:

> They were two very depressing days. An hour before we were to go to bid farewell to our dog, I set out to do some shopping. I walked along very gloomily, almost in tears, when, suddenly – and it really was like a bolt from the blue, for my stomach contracted just as if I had received a blow – I *knew* the dog would recover. I turned and ran back home and told my husband, and he phoned the vet at once. We were told that Jack had just stood up and, although somewhat stiffly, was actually walking again. That was six years ago, and now Jack is a plump old dog, but as jolly and good tempered as ever.

Since then Jack has gone the way of all dogs, but the unusual rapport which made him and the family of which he was a part, is well remembered, like the curious, telepathic *knowledge* that he was not dying but had been given a new lease of life.

Mrs Sylvia Fisher, a parapsychologist who studied the subject at Blue Ridge Community College in Weyers Cave, Virginia, USA, decided recently to extend her researches into the alleged telepathic capacity of dogs. The route by which she arrived at her decision was a little unusual. She began in the first instance by buying six philodendrons at her local stores, and, on the fast-growing belief that plants behave better or grow healthier if they are loved and fussed over, she named two of them Venus and Leda, after two dogs she loved, and called two other plants 'hate plants', naming them after two dogs she disliked. All six plants were lined up next to each other on the kitchen windowsill and given exactly the same treatment – the same amount of water every day. Venus and Leda prospered, growing taller and faster. Poor Tippy and Kenny, the 'unloved' plants which were 'subject to bad thoughts' (she said nice things to Venus and Leda), were decidedly inferior to the luckier pair. Okie and Dusty, the remaining pair, were absolutely ignored. From this Mrs Fisher concluded that loved plants grow healthiest.

This foray into psychic research sparked off her interest in dogs and telepathy. She found she could send mental commands to a dog. She would mentally order her labrador, Trooper, to come to her and in sixty-four experiments found that this 'telepathy to order' worked in over half the cases. Interestingly enough, this proportion of successes was similar to that achieved by Dr Durov in Russia just before, and after, World War I.

2

Dogs and ESP

> They haven't got no noses,
> The fallen sons of Eve . . .
> 'The Song of Quoodle', G. K. Chesterton

Quoodle, Chesterton's archetypal dog, goes on to list all the natural smells that man with his blunted senses misses, among them 'the brilliant smell of water, the brave smell of a stone, the smell of dew and thunder'. Then, Quoodle adds, there is 'the smell of snare and warning', an abstract concept which suggests that more than mere 'noselessness' is involved. In effect, Chesterton is posing the question: have dogs extra-sensory perception? By which is meant gifts and faculties beyond scientific explanation in the state of our present knowledge. Or, as Chesterton-cum-Quoodle put it,

> More than mind discloses
> And more than men believe.

We do not know a great deal about the workings of the human brain, while the word 'mind', which we use constantly, is an abstraction; nobody has ever isolated or identified a 'mind'. We know even less about the workings of the thought-processes of animals. We see only the symptoms of their emotions and moods and needs. It is not easy to specify what is normal or abnormal in animal behaviour, but it seems certain that animals, and dogs especially, have powers which may reasonably be described as supernatural, or psychic. Captain A. H. Trapman, whose book *The Dog* is a well-known classic by a man who spent his life studying their nature and habits, had absolutely no doubt of what he described as the 'supernatural attributes' of dogs. Not only is the link between dog and man a mystery, but in its workings it produces many other mysteries.

Since Captain Trapman wrote his book, over half a century ago, the supernatural attributes of dogs have come under the close scrutiny of scientists, animal behaviourists, parapsychologists and psychologists. There have been many examples, in fairly clearly defined categories of phenomena, affecting dogs. These categories are 'psi-trailing' (orientation by unexplained means); dogs sensitive to occult or psychic phenomena; dogs appearing as spectres; dogs receiving telepathic messages, or even consciously or unconsciously conveying information over a long distance to their owners; or being able to foresee disasters and taking evasive action; and, foreseeing danger to their owners, managing to dissuade them from courses which would have proved fatal. Nowadays we call the propensity by which one is aware of something that will happen in the future 'precognition', and I shall use the term in that sense to indicate that dogs are certainly precognitive.

Let us consider *precognition* – seeming knowledge of the future – first, keeping a clear distinction between that and a dog's capacity to know that something has happened far away at the moment that it has happened. The latter is also an interesting phenomenon but is not precognition.

Captain Trapman describes how, during the First World War, a dog gave a striking display of premonition. The Airedale's master was a naval officer on mine-sweeping duty in the North Sea. His wife lived in Harwich, which was his headquarters, and both she and the dog would go down to the quayside to see him off on his numerous expeditions. He was a cheerful and matter-of-fact officer, not given to nerves or misgivings, and accepted the risks inherent in his work with the philosophy of the serving man. The Airedale had never shown the slightest sign of distress when seeing him off, as though confident, as both of them were, that there would be a reunion again soon.

Yet, on the last night the officer was to spend on land, the dog behaved in an erratic and entirely uncharacteristic manner. At the quayside and on board the dog persistently tried to dissuade his master from sailing, tugging at his trousers, pulling at his sleeves, dragging at his coat, whimpering and showing distress.

That night the officer was drowned and his ship lost. At the approximate time he drowned (nobody survived to time it with certainty, but it was known within ten minutes) the dog howled inconsolably.

In the middle of last century, the case of a dog foreseeing a shipwreck aroused great interest. The *Beaufoy* packet ship, carrying mail from Cuxhaven, Germany to Britain, ran into a terrible storm – lightning, thunder and winds reaching gale force. Captain Norris had with him a favourite dog which had accompanied him on many a voyage and was well used to the moods of the sea. Indeed, the dog was usually very reluctant to leave the vessel which it regarded as its home.

During this storm, however, its behaviour changed from the start of the voyage; it would jump overboard and swim towards another mail-boat. This it did several times until, in exasperation, the captain gave orders that it should be confined.

It would seem that the dog had a presentiment of catastrophe, for almost immediately a tremendous wave struck the vessel, tearing away the bulwark, to which the captain and three of his men were clinging, the mast, stanchions and everything on deck. All sank, but one sole survivor was lucky in that the receding surge thrust him back to what remained of the damaged vessel which, buffeted about in the stormy seas, was at last towed into the Weser by a Heligoland boat.

It seems that dogs can sense not only general events but actions contemplated by human beings, especially crimes. One classic case concerns Sir Henry Lee, ancestor of the earls of Lichfield, who had as a watchdog a huge mastiff which was feared not only by the entire household but by his own master, who only kept him for his aggressive appearance. Fierce the dog might have been, but he proved loyal enough.

Sir Henry had engaged a new member of the household staff – a confidential valet, whose duties would take him into and about his master's bedroom. The man was an Italian, and his arrival on the scene caused the dog to behave in a very strange and unprecedented manner. Instead of roaming at will throughout the household, curling up to sleep lightly, where he chose, ready for the slightest sound, the dog followed master and valet up to the master's bedroom and even entered the room, which was out of bounds. He was instantly thrown out but scratched violently at the closed door, howling constantly.

Sir Henry instructed the valet to send the dog away, but the dog would take no orders from the valet and kept returning and creating such a commotion that for the sake of peace and quiet Sir Henry relented and let the animal into his bedroom. He was in fact touched and surprised at this unaccustomed show of affection. As he let the dog in, it wagged its tail madly and, crawling under his master's bed, lay down there. The valet withdrew.

In the silence of the night the door creaked open. Sir Henry awoke and at the same instant his dog sprang upon the intruder and pinned him down. In the pitch dark, as the intruder roared with fear and begged for assistance, Sir Henry came over and grappled with him, to find it was his newly engaged valet. The valet apologized profusely, trying to explain away his intrusion, but his excuses sounded so unlikely (he had not been summoned, nor had any of his allotted duties been neglected before he retired) that Sir Henry, now thoroughly suspicious, ordered the valet to be taken before a magistrate. Immediately the valet was contrite and, begging for mercy, confessed that it had been his intention to kill his master, then rob the house.

Only the dog's prescience and insistence upon an unaccustomed action had saved his master's life. Sir Henry had never imagined that the fierce-looking dog he maintained as a protector had such intelligence and such affection for him. He commissioned a full-length portrait of himself to be painted, showing the mastiff at his side and bearing the grateful inscription 'More faithful than favoured'.

Numerous books and thousands of articles have been written about Jack the Ripper, a Victorian murderer who killed several street-women in Whitechapel, in London's notorious East End, between 31 August and 8 November 1888. His habit of mutilating his victims with surgical precision sent shivers of horror through London; but despite the citizens' vigilance, he was never captured and his identity was never established. Today's speculations are inconclusive.

Even so, Mrs T. P. O'Connor relates a strange story of how her dog identified, and nearly caught, the murderer. Attracted by the mystery, as many other Victorian ladies were, she could not resist driving with a friend, accompanied by her dog, to the spot where murder had been committed. Her dog Max behaved strangely, showing excitement and distress. It was ill at ease even when they had returned home, and ran out at the first opportunity, disappearing into the night. Mrs O'Connor was much relieved when a nightwatchman turned up with the dog, whose name and address were on his collar. The watchman said a stranger had brought the dog to him. He described the man, and his description sounds very eery indeed: 'Looked like he might have been Jack the Ripper himself! His skin was green-white, just the colour of the stomach of a frog. He didn't have a drop of red blood in him, and his fingers were tough white roots. He was a rum customer, he was, and yet Max wanted to follow him.' It appeared that, while the dog had been shut up in the watchman's hut, he had set up a dismal howling – and it turned out that this was just about the time Jack the Ripper was murdering two more women near the site of the original crime. Did Max, when he escaped from the O'Connor home, seek out the murderer near the site Mrs O'Connor had taken him to, and was the unpleasant-looking stranger who handed him over to the nightwatchman Jack the Ripper, anxious to be rid of a troublesome witness? Mrs T. P. O'Connor thought this likely.

Just as dogs have often demonstrated a sense of premonition, so, by some unexplained faculty, they are often aware of impending death, even when this is being enacted some distance – even a vast distance – away. And, by what appears to be something akin to telepathy, they are often aware that something is happening to their owner at the very time of the occurrence.

Captain Trapman knew of many instances where dogs, left behind by their owners, knew before the event that their masters would meet disaster. One widow described to him how, on the morning of 15 September 1915, she was surprised not to receive her accustomed greeting from her pet dog, Bob. Bob normally slept on the mat just inside her bedroom, and when she awoke he would jump on the bed, lick her face and wag his tail. But on this morning she had to call twice before the dog crawled listlessly from underneath her bed, licked her hand briefly and crawled miserably back again into the shadows. He stayed under the bed, refusing both food and his accustomed walk.

Thinking the dog was ill, his owner took him to the vet, who could find nothing amiss. On returning home the dog lay as though glued to the mat, looking the picture of melancholy. While his owner was wondering whether a second visit to the vet was necessary, he sat up on his haunches and howled mournfully.

Four days later the woman heard that her husband had been killed in action on the night of 15 September. Two years later a brother officer told her how her husband had died. He had been shot going 'over the top' and, allowing for differences in clock time due to distance, the dog had begun his howling at just that moment, at the 'zero hour' of the attack. It would seem to have been telepathic contact which made the dog howl at the moment of death – and to have been an instance of precognition that the dog was disconsolate and troubled for several hours beforehand.

Mr Frank Ashworth, a retired Bank of England official now living in Fowey, Cornwall, has described to me how a dog seemed to know that his mother was about to die. As he told me:

I took an early pension from the Bank of England, and though my wife was still working, we decided to keep a dog. We acquired a black and tan miniature dachshund, called Mitzi. We had a flat in Maidenhead. But I was travelling regularly down to Fowey and back, and after a few months, we thought the dog might be lonely. We placed an advertisement in the *Maidenhead Advertiser* and heard of Heidi, who had been picked up as a stray and was in the RSPCA kennels at Slough. While basically a dachshund, she is crossed with some sort of terrier . . .

I went over to see her and introduced her to Mitzi. They seemed to get on well, and two days later I collected her. She settled down very well.

At this time (July 1974) my mother was living at Leigh-on-Sea and we always took the dogs when visiting her. She took to Heidi immediately and vice versa. The rapport seemed to grow. Anyway, in October, Mother left Leigh-on-Sea and came to live in a flat across the Court from us.

I used to go over on most days . . . Mother always gave Heidi a piece of apple. If we were there for any length of time, she would curl up on Mother's lap.

On 5 December Mother was taken ill and deteriorated during the day, so one of us stayed over there. That night nothing untoward happened, but on the Friday she had a stroke which was to prove fatal within twenty-four hours.

During that day, Heidi was a little restless, but we put it down to unusual surroundings. However, when it came to night time, she would not settle for more than a few minutes at a time, which was most unusual. Both my wife and I commented that she must know something was wrong. The dog was up and down off a chair, into the basket, on our laps, and so on. This continued until about eleven o'clock next morning, when suddenly Heidi jumped off the chair, onto the bed and licked my mother's hands and wrists and all over her face as though it were a last loving lick. Within an hour Mother died and after an hour or so Heidi settled down to normality.

Mr Tim Minogue of Clarendon Park, Leicester, tells me of a similar instance, which he heard from a farmer he knew. The farmer's father, a very old man, had a dog which was his constant companion. It followed him everywhere, and always showed the liveliest delight when spoken to or whenever it met him after an absence, however short. When the old farmer returned from work, the dog would be 'all over him', but one day it failed to give his master his accustomed greeting and, stranger still, completely ignored him, almost as though he was not there. After dinner the old man sat down in his favourite chair. The dog still ignored him, and refused offers of food. An hour after sitting himself in the chair, the old man died. The farmer's son maintained that his father's spirit had already left his body and that, therefore, the dog did not recognize him. The idea that the spirit leaves the body before death is still quite common in some country districts of England. Whatever the explanation, it would seem that the dog had some premonition of his master's death.

Dogs not only have a premonition of the death of somebody they love, but in one recent case even averted that death. Frank

Mattingley, of West End, Southampton, owes his life to Tipper, the border Collie who has been his friend and companion for years.

In 1984 Mr Mattingley was admitted to Southampton General Hospital after collapsing with a mystery illness. His condition deteriorated rapidly and he was in a coma. At one point he was so ill that doctors were surprised he lasted one night. They advised his wife, Kathleen, to call the family together.

One son, a seaman, flew in from Holland to be with the others at his bedside. They tried talking to him in the hope of awakening him to consciousness. Nothing worked. Then somebody heard him whisper Tipper's name. The dog was brought to the hospital and tethered a floor below the ward on a flat roof. Frank's bed and all the monitoring equipment were pushed towards the ward window.

The dog's reaction amazed everybody. He started barking and howling frantically and tried to climb up the wall. At that point Mr Mattingley started talking. 'Everyone was amazed,' says Mr Mattingley: 'It was though I had come back from the dead.'

The hospital staff deserve all credit for the prompt and intelligent way they suggested that the dog should be brought to hospital. The almost magical link between dog and man had once again asserted itself.

From Illinois, USA, a case was reported where a sheepdog belonging to Francis McMahon knew when its master had died. When McMahon went into hospital with a fractured skull after a fall, the dog followed him and waited on the steps. At the moment its master passed away, the dog began continuous and inconsolate howling. Furthermore, the dog would not leave the spot. Until it died, twelve years later, Shep was to be found on the hospital stairs.

Dr Ute Pleimes, of the University of Giessen, West Germany, has for many years collected and investigated instances of ESP in animals. She holds that more attention should be paid to their forewarnings of disaster. She gives the instance of a woman who ignored her dog's warning when it might have saved her life. The woman had borrowed a neighbour's car. The neighbour's dog did everything in his power to stop her driving away, growling angrily, trying to snatch the keys from her hand. She had a job to shake the dog off and as she drove away, the dog followed, yelping, until he was out-distanced. An hour later the car skidded and hit a wall. The woman was killed instantly.

Another case concerned Josef Becker, who went for a stroll with his Alsatian, Strulli, and looked in at a local inn in Saar Louis. The dog became agitated, doing everything possible to attract attention, running round in circles, howling at his master, tugging at his clothes and trying to drag him from his seat. Strulli was such a nuisance that Becker, intent on his drink and convivial company, put the dog outside and shut the door.

Somehow the dog got into the inn by another entrance and began to tug frantically at Becker's clothes. Tired of this losing battle and seeing that he would never enjoy his drink in peace, Becker left the inn at two minutes to five. Two minutes later, to the deafening crash of timber, bricks and plaster, the inn collapsed on its occupants, killing nine people and injuring over twenty others.

Strulli the Alsatian had some powerful premonition of disaster and, by his persistence, saved his master's life. Builders excavating next door had damaged the inn's foundations. Nobody suspected it, but the dog knew something was wrong.

Forewarning of disaster saved a family from death, according to a report in the *Sunday People* in 1974. A Leicester reader described how their dog started howling and jumping around in the car in so unusual a way that they stopped the car and took him for a walk. When they returned to the car, they realized that something was wrong with the front wheel. A mechanic they called kicked the wheel off. The axle had totally snapped. Had they driven on and tackled the steep hill not far ahead, they would most probably all have been killed.

The *Watford Evening Echo* in January 1971 published a story about a five-year-old Collie, Laddie, who accompanied his master every day to the slate quarry where he worked. This had been the dog's habit ever since he was a puppy, but one morning he refused to budge from the house. Nothing would persuade him to move, and for the first time his master, Robert Hayes, went to work alone. Just before midday there was an explosion in the quarry. Hayes was killed and two others were seriously injured. What explanation can there be other than that the dog knew what would happen?

Dr J. Gaither Pratt of the Department of Psychiatry, University of Virginia, Charlottesville, USA, a distinguished parapsychologist who assisted Dr J. B. Rhine in his trail-blazing research into extra-sensory perception, has described a case of 'distant knowledge' or telepathy which came to his attention: 'I heard the mother of a family in New Jersey tell about how their pet dog suddenly went under the house and started whining, a continuous crying. This was the only time the dog had ever acted in this way, and they were not able to call him out or get him to stop his strange barking. Later in the day news came that the older son of the family had been killed in an automobile accident on the way home from college, and the time of his death coincided with the beginning of the dog's unusual behaviour.'

A reader of the old London *Daily News* described how, in 1920, her husband went to Romania to work for his firm. At the time they had a Sealyham called Michael, who was devoted to him. Late one evening, a few days after his master had gone, the dog was run over just outside the gate of their home. He was dying and lay in her arms until the veterinary surgeon arrived and decided that the only merciful thing was to put him to sleep.

She knew that her husband would be terribly upset at the loss of the pet he loved so much and, knowing of the new responsibilities and problems he would be encountering in Romania, decided to keep the bad news until he returned home. Here, in her own words, is what happened:

> Some days later I heard from him. I have the letter still. What follows is copied from it:
> 'An odd thing happened Tuesday night. I was in a stopping train near Sinaia. Girl got in – rum-looking girl – great green eyes – got to work with the lipstick as soon as she sat down. Presently she said, in broken English:
> '"The small white dog, the English dog, is he not the dog of monsieur?"
> '"What dog?" I said.

'She pointed into the corridor.
' *"Dehors."* [Outside.]
    'I got up and looked out. There was nothing there. First move in the friendly game, thought I, and shut up pretty quickly. At the next stop she got out. After that I dozed off, but was awakened suddenly by a dog scratching at the door – sounded for all the world like Micky outside the bathroom in the morning. I jumped out, half asleep, but there was nothing there. I could have sworn it was Micky. Is he all right? . . .'
Tuesday was the night Micky lay dying in my arms in Oxford.

This account of the dying Sealyham brought a similar account of a 'ghost' of a dog appearing to its owners at the moment of death:

    Reading the account of the dying Sealyham made me think that the unaccountable experience I had last week may not have been imagination. We had a lovely terrier dog whose one and only fault was chasing motor cars and bicycles. Last Thursday evening she was run over at the other end of the town. The lady whose car knocked her down, although she was quite blameless in the matter, picked poor Tiny up and raced from one end of the town to the other to find a vet to take the dog in. As its collar was lost a day or two before, and the one it had on had no name on it, they had no means of letting us know where Tiny was. My brother and daughter followed one clue after another when searching for the dog, and eventually found it at a vet's place quite near our house. The surgeon could not say then how much she was hurt, but quite thought that she would recover.
    On Friday morning my daughter went again to see Tiny. The poor creature knew her, but the vet said she must leave her till Saturday as she was unable to stand. About four in the afternoon, my daughter and I heard a loud scratching on the street door. We both said 'That's Tiny.' We rushed to the door, but there was no dog in sight. I told my brother, and he said he thought he heard her whine, but added that all our nerves were jarred and we fancied things. On Saturday, when my daughter went again to the vet, he told her that tiny, later in the day on Friday, had become paralysed and he had to put her to sleep as there was no hope for her. . .

These last two accounts suggest that animals (in this instance, dogs) may possess the capacity now generally described as 'astral projection' – where the soul, or the psyche, or whatever name one cares to attach to a personality presumed to exist separately from the body but within the body during the latter's life, projects itself. A British scientist, Dr Robert Crookall, collected hundreds of such cases in respect of human beings. Does something similar happen with dogs? Or are there *ghosts* of dogs?

The archives of ghost stories, which are considerable, include very many in which the ghosts of dogs are alleged to have been seen.

Lady Dowding, widow of Air Chief Marshal Lord Dowding, the Battle of Britain hero, relates what happened to her son David when he was a child. He had been brought up with a Highland terrier to which he was greatly attached. One of the dog's favourite tricks was tucking his head down and spinning round on his feet, an antic which always gave the boy great amusement. When the dog, called Doggy Day, died, David claimed that he often still saw him. He told his mother: 'It's a peculiar thing. When Doggy Day comes now, I never see his head. He just spins round in circles by my feet.'

The *Review of Reviews* of 5 December 1890 contains an extraordinary account of a ghostly dog which actually *bit* an observer! It being a somewhat lengthy and detailed account, here is just a summary of it.

Mr James Durham was the nightwatchman of Britain's first railway station – the old Darlington and Stockton Station. One bitterly cold night he sought the comfort and warmth of a porter's cellar, where there was an open coal fire and a coal-house leading from the cellar. He went down the steps, took off his overcoat and sat on a bench opposite the fire. He lit the gas-bracket and had just sat down when he was surprised to see a strange man come out of the coal-house, followed by a big black retriever. The stranger gave no sort of greeting or acknowledgement. From the outset his behaviour was peculiar. He fixed his eye upon the watchman, never taking his gaze from him, and moved in front of the fire. The watchman, puzzled and a trifle suspicious, watched him intently, too. Then, as Mr Durham related to W. T. Stead who, at the time, edited the influential *Pall Mall Gazette*:

There he stood looking at me, and a curious smile came over his countenance. He had a stand-up collar and a cut-away coat with gilt buttons and a Scotch cap. All at once he struck at me, and I had the impression that he hit me. I up with my fist and struck back at him. My fist seemed to go through him and struck against the stone of the fireplace, and knocked the skin off my knuckles. *Immediately the dog gripped me by the calf of my leg, and seemed to cause me pain.* The man recovered his position, called off the dog with a sort of click of the tongue, then went back into the coal-house, followed by the dog. I lighted my dark lantern and looked into the coal-house, but there was neither man nor dog, and no outlet for them except the one by which they had entered.

When Mr Durham related his alarming experience, it caused a local sensation. The railway owner, Edward Pease, sent for him and listened to his account, as did his three sons. Durham was closely questioned and able to assure them that he had not been asleep, that he was in no disturbed or distraught state of mind and – being a teetotaller – was certainly not the worse for drink. Indeed, he had not touched a drop of drink for forty-nine years. It transpired that, a number of years before, a man employed in the station office had committed suicide, and his body had been carried into the same cellar in which Mr Durham sought refuge from the cold. Further, Mr Pease assured him that the description of the apparition exactly fitted that of the dead employee, who had owned a black retriever similar to that which had bitten Mr Durham.

A former chief constable of Warwickshire, in his memoirs published in 1821, mentions a haunted house where a large grey dog was frequently seen in company with a phantom whose 'face' was a shapeless blob. One gas-fitter saw the apparition no fewer than nine times. Local legend ascribed the hauntings to the fact that some body-snatchers, preferring, like Burke and Hare, to secure live victims and then killing them before selling their bodies to medical students, had lured their victims to the house. Callers were often seen going in, but not coming out.

In the *Book of Days*, published last century, a correspondent described how a chimney-sweep murdered by drowning an old woman he suspected of witchcraft. He was hanged in chains near to the scene of his crime, and thereafter, so it was said, the spot was haunted by a large, black, spectral dog, 'as big as a Newfoundland, but very gaunt, shaggy, with long ears and tail, eyes like balls of fire and large, long teeth, for he opened his mouth and seemed to grin at us. In a few minutes the dog disappeared, seeming to vanish like a shadow, or to sink into the earth, and we drove over the spot where he had lain.'

A correspondent once described to the late Elliott O'Donnell, author of many books on ghosts and the occult (in *Animal Ghosts*, Rider, 1913) how, on going down what he calls H--- Street (which I take to be Harley Street from all the other details given) he found himself at first followed and then led by a ghostly dachshund which stopped at a particular house, looked round at him as though inviting action and then vanished!

A second correspondent came up with a story which in O'Donnell's opinion not only amplified but confirmed and explained the whole occurrence. This lady had owned a dachshund which disappeared, causing her to search for it persistently and constantly. Her husband was an oculist, and they lived near the spot in which the ghostly dog had been seen. Passing through the area, she saw her dog ahead of her, looking at her with 'sad, brown eyes' and, strangely enough, soaked and muddy although the weather was hot and dry. The dog moved at a steady pace ahead of her, and she tried unsuccessfully to overtake it. It stopped outside the house where the ghost had been seen by the other correspondent, then 'glided through the stone steps into the area'.

Exploring the area, the woman noticed that a piece of raw meat had been left in a low wooden box. Why was it there? To tempt dogs? She enquired at the house but got a brusque reception from the servant who answered the door. Enquiring elsewhere, she found that the house was occupied by a hospital research worker engaged in vivisection.

Stories of ghostly dogs are very numerous in England. Ghostly black dogs have at various times been reported in Stogursey, a ruined monastery in north Somerset, Weacombe in the Quantocks, Winsford Hill and on the sea road from St Audries to Perry Farm in Somerset. Mr Frank Glanville, a Porlock magistrate, told the *Somerset County Gazette* of 'a large dog-like animal' whose appearances on two occasions had coincided with a local death.

Spiritualists accept the survival of animals as a fact, and there are numerous accounts of dogs greeting their former owners with recognizable barks and noises at séances. That phantasms of dogs have been seen is not arguable, unless one rejects the veracity of a very large number of people from all walks of life, including a considerable number who had actually something to lose by disclosing their experiences – whose accounts might, let us say, single them out as eccentric or credulous.

Without speculating as to whether phantasms of dogs have any objective reality (in other words, whether they are impressions only or would still exist if unseen by an observer), I believe that the accounts add up to one significant fact: that animals too possess psyches and that, as with human beings, their emotions are not necessarily ephemeral. I have always been convinced that thought, which involves brain processes, does not disappear the moment the thought has taken place. Even more so, I think, is this true of intense emotion, which may be likened to a concentrated and unusually powerful thought process. I have always maintained that thoughts can leave their impress on so-called 'inanimate' things.

Thought and emotion involve mental energy. Mental energy involves electricity. The human brain has between twelve and fourteen billion cells with a combined electrical power of a hundred watts. The electrical impulses of the brain are easily recorded by the electro-encephalograph.

That the brain emits electrical energy – however faint the impulses – is unarguable. On what basis, however, is one entitled to assert that mental energy can affect matter? The answer is that matter is comprised of molecules, which are built up of atoms. Each atom is a whirling, minute universe of energy, with a nucleus of protons and neutrons around which electrons circulate at tremendous speed. One theory propounds that mental energy can affect the behaviour of electrons. If this is true, it would mean that material things can be affected by mental energy. It is not merely possible but highly probable that this energy leaves its impress on buildings, objects and places. These impressions may be picked up by others, producing the phenomena we know as ghosts and hauntings. If the mental energy of human beings is recorded in this way, the same may hold true with animals.

Apart from being seen as apparitions, dogs are on record as reacting to apparitions, or to haunted places, as seeing apparitions, hearing ghostly sounds or sensing the sinister atmosphere. For instance, the Connaught Arms, in East London, is said to be haunted by the ghost of a mad woman who committed suicide there. A member of the staff once entered the room in which she died to find it in complete chaos and, as he left the room, was confronted by a wild-looking woman whose fierce looks sent his two dogs scampering away in terror – he tried to outdo them in speed! Dogs have been known to recoil in terror at the ghost said to haunt the Grenadier pub at Hyde Park Corner in London. The spectre is believed to be that of a guards officer who was flogged to death by his brother officers after being found cheating at cards. Geoffrey Bernerd, the landlord, who sometimes stays at the Grenadier with his wife, tells me that he has often heard loud, distinct raps on the door upstairs, at a time when nobody could be upstairs.

Mrs Barbara Kipling, of Leamington Spa, Warwickshire, the wife of a doctor, has reported to me an interesting case of a dog reacting to a haunted site. It happened in June 1976. With her husband, she went with members of the local literary society to visit Burton Dassett church, built on the ridge neighbouring Edgehill, about eleven miles south of Warwick. When the meeting had disbanded, they let their dog (an old Jack Russell terrier) out of the car for a run on the top of the ridge.

For the first minute or so the dog was absolutely delighted and started rabbit-hunting. Then, suddenly, she stopped in her tracks, stock still, coat bristling 'and ran for her life away from us, with her tail between her legs. We had difficulty in catching her. We thought perhaps that she had been stung.'

Three days later the Kiplings again visited the site, because their grandson wanted to fly a kite on Burton Dassett Hill. They had forgotten their dog's strange behaviour and were absorbed with their grandson's efforts to get his kite airborne when they observed their dog behaving in exactly the same strange way. The dog 'seemed really distressed, and when we caught her, trembled and gasped until we were well away from the hill'.

The spot where the dog reacted in this way was a Saxon burial place where, a few years ago, forty skeletons were discovered, dating back to the sixth century. This is, incidentally, near the spot where the Battle of Edgehill was fought in 1642 – and, to the amazement and fear of the residents, was re-enacted by ghostly soldiers, complete with the noise of gunfire, the neighing of horses and cries of the wounded, on Christmas Eve following the battle. Everything looked real – the Cavaliers and Roundheads, the horses, the guns – while the din made it seem that the whole thing had started all over again. So many people swore to what they had seen and heard that King Charles sent three officers to investigate. The investigators confirmed the truth of the stories and even claimed to have recognized the ghosts of some of the Cavaliers killed at Edgehill! The ghostly fighters have been seen by many people since.

This was the area where the Kiplings' dog was so terrified. As human beings have seen ghosts there, perhaps the dog did too.

A case of a dog which 'certainly saw a ghost' has been described to me by a correspondent living at Milton Lilbourne, near Pewsey, Wiltshire. With her dog, a terrier called Chipmunk, she was on a visit to Wooton Courtenay, near Minehead. 'My dog,' she recalls, 'was sitting by my side when he suddenly got up barking and twice, still barking wildly, arched his back, evidently avoiding a (friendly?) hand, as dogs do at times. He kept up his barking for about ten minutes. Months later I learned that the house was haunted by two women, a mother and her daughter.' This was the only occasion on which her dog behaved in this unusual way, taking aggressive action as though avoiding an invisible presence.

An unusual case of a dog greeting an invisible person was related to me recently by Mrs Vivienne Smalley of Stafford Road, Cannock, Staffordshire. An Airedale used to sleep in his master's room and was there when his master died. She was asked to look after the dog during the funeral. She told me: 'I took him for a walk over the heath, and suddenly, for no apparent reason, he dashed ahead, wagged his tail and went up on his hind legs just as if he was reaching up to his master's chest.'

It may be that animals owned by particular people, or with people having psychic sensibility or insight, see and know things by some process of telepathy. This would explain to some extent the fact that several unusual instances occur to the same owner. This happened to Mrs Smalley, when another dog which she encountered seemed to respond to some psychic influence or phenomenon. She was living in an old cottage in Heatherton Cannock, Staffordshire, with a red setter bitch, which she considers 'amongst the more sensitive of dogs'. The cottage in the next field, known locally as Stacey's Field, was demolished because an old shepherd had hanged himself there, and it was now reputed to be haunted. When it was down to the ground, her dog became restless and agitated, moving constantly from one corner of the room to another, sometimes moving to an inglenook, staring and growling with her back hair up. Nothing Mrs Smalley could do would pacify her, so after sitting up with her until three o'clock in the morning, she gave her three aspirins and nursed her to sleep. She continues: 'When I got up in the morning she was in the corner fast asleep. Suddenly she awakened and made one dash outside and over to the ruined cottage.' This happened on another night, by which time Mrs Smalley was convinced that the ghost of the shepherd was haunting the spot. Not being frightened of such things, though convinced that ghosts could be a reality, she went to the spot and 'told the shepherd to go away'. That was the end of this kind of disturbance.

Miss P. C. Storey, of Rosecroft Avenue, London, tells me of two experiences in which her dog, Simon, seemed to sense an unseen presence. Her sister was playing the piano in the drawing-room of their family home in Eastbourne when the dog suddenly started barking and gaping up at a small divan beside the mantelpiece. He was told to shut up but continued barking and backing away after yet another advance, as though a stranger was there whom he was actively trying to 'see off'. Impatiently, since the noise interrupted her music, the sister rolled a ball to the dog to distract him. Only for a split second was the dog diverted, stopping to stare and bark at the divan. Then, after a pause, he sniffed along the edge and underneath the seat as if to check on who or what had been there.

The files of the Society for Psychical Research in Britain, and its American counterpart, contain hundreds of such cases, proving that dogs possess unusual sensitivity and perception, often to a degree which fully justifies the description ESP.

3

The Homing Instinct

One day in 1973 Willem Mante, master of a Dutch freighter, *S.S. Simaloer*, was waiting on board at Vancouver, impatient to weigh anchor and proceed on the next long hop of the journey to Japan.

He was puzzled and troubled, for Hector, his pet terrier which had sailed the world with him, had not returned to the ship. When the ship was in port, Hector had broken loose and gone to explore the town. This was his usual pleasure, yet he had never failed to come padding up the gangplank shortly before the ship was due to sail. Nobody ever knew, or could guess, how he always found his way about strange towns, through the labyrinth of streets and alleys and steps, yet until now he had always retraced his course to that point in the harbour where the ship was berthed, at the right time.

At last, sadly, Willem Mante decided he could wait no longer. His dog had either met with an accident or been stolen or got lost. He never expected to see him again.

The next morning an officer on another Vancouver-docked ship, *S.S. Hanley*, saw a wire-haired terrier walk up the gangplank of his vessel. The dog seemed intent on some mission, not just wandering at random. He trotted around the deck, went below to sniff at the cargo and then left.

The same thing was observed by the crews of three other vessels in harbour. Hector had boarded the vessels, looked speedily but thoroughly around and then disembarked and disappeared.

Only when the Yokohama-bound *S.S. Hanley* was two hours out of port was Hector found on board. Nineteen days later, as the ship approached Japan, the canine stowaway became noticeably restless and, as the ship entered Tokyo, was literally shivering with excitement.

During the unloading of the *Hanley*'s cargo, another vessel moved into a berth about 300 yards away, and some men from the newly arrived steamer sailed in a sampan near the *Hanley*'s stern. As the small craft approached, Captain Kildall, of the *Hanley*, noticed the dog's excitement and cries. Suddenly the dog jumped into the water, a few feet from the sampan, swam to it and was pulled aboard, throwing himself at one of the crew, yelping with delight and wagging his tail furiously. Miracle or not, Hector had found his master – and travelled over 5,000 miles to do it.

What puzzled the overjoyed Mante was how the dog knew *which* vessel to choose at Vancouver. How did he know the *Hanley* was Japan-bound? 'There is no logical explanation,' was all Mante could say. 'We can't account for it. We can only marvel at the fact that it really happened.'

The dog's patience, sagacity, devotion and courage can be understood; dogs have long demonstrated these qualities, even though we never cease to marvel at them. But more impressive and mysterious is the dog's capacity to seek out and find his owner, or some place to which it wishes to return. By what means it can do this nobody really knows, not even after decades of research. Dogs will make their way through streets they have never seen, cross rivers, traverse mountains. We could, with fair accuracy, call this phenomenon 'the homing instinct', except that we have no proof that it is an instinct. We merely know that it happens and that an assessment of a dog's known capacities does nothing to explain it. The dog's scent is about a thousand times as acute as that of a human being, but this would not account for a dog finding its way over unfamiliar territory over which its master has travelled by train, boat or car. This is the phenomenon which we now call ESP and which Dr Rhine called 'psi-trailing' in the course of a research programme for the Duke Laboratory, which in 1950 began its survey to decide whether animals have psychic capacities. There existed already, in numerous libraries and private collections, an impressive accumulation of well-authenticated stories indicative of unusual capacities in animals, but there had not hitherto been a controlled, statistical and severely scientific approach to this subject, except for the work conducted since 1882 by the Society for Psychical Research.

For convenience the cases were divided into three principal categories: (1) migration of birds, insects and certain marine animals; (2) experiments in the homing behaviour of mice, cats, pigeons, dogs and other living creatures; and (3) stories of unusual animal behaviour covering a wide spectrum of assorted phenomena.

Associated with Dr Rhine in this programme were Dr Karl Otis and Dr J. Gaither Pratt, whom I have mentioned elsewhere in connection with 'psi-trailing' cats.

As a result of publicity by the laboratory, over 500 'anecdotal' cases were reported and later investigated in what was called the ANPSI project (coined from 'animals' and 'psi'). It did not take long to discern that there were five principal categories of behaviour involved: (1) behaviour suggestive of impending danger to the animal itself or its master; (2) behaviour suggestive of an animal's knowledge of danger to its master at a distance; (3) anticipation of a master's return; (4) homing behaviour and (5) 'psi-trailing' behaviour.

It is this last category which concerns me for the moment, and the example I have quoted above, of Willem Mante and his dog Hector, is one reported recently, long after ANPSI carried out its pioneering work. It proved to be one of the most dramatic, as well as the most puzzling, phenomena with which Dr Rhine and his colleagues had to deal.

In their investigations, Dr Rhine devised criteria by which conscious or unconscious deception could be ruled out and where fact could clearly and conclusively be separated from rumour. I have investigated a good many alleged psychic occurrences and strange stories and have tried, by commonsense standards, to eliminate dubious or ambiguous accounts. Thus, one has to ask: is the informant a responsible person – with a record of veracity, somebody with no ulterior motive? Are the witnesses or corroborators of equal probity? Does the informant have any physical handicap which might give him distorted vision or hearing? And were any notes made at the appropriate time?

As regards psi-trailing, it is clearly necessary to establish that the animal credited with marvellous and seemingly impossible journeys is one and the same. Was the dog that arrived of the same sex, size, colour and breed, and were any special peculiarities of marking, or physical identifications, such as a healed wound or torn ear, checked? The colour of the animal's eyes, even the length of the hair, has to be noted. Comparisons of photographs (of the animal that was owned and the animal that arrived) are an obvious help. Although most dog-owners will insist that they know their own pet and that their pet knows them, in a scientific evaluation such care on matters of detail are essential if other people are to be convinced.

Twenty-eight cases concerning dogs were investigated in the course of this project.

One case reported was that of 'Old Taylor', a Tennessee farm dog, which pined when the farmer's son went to Washington College, about a hundred miles away, accompanied by his mother and sister, who set up house for him there, leaving only the farmer and his dog on the farm. 'Old Taylor' was greatly attached to the lad and on Thanksgiving Day appeared, whining and scratching, at the front door of the residence the family had established at the college.

It was the farmer's turn to feel lonely. His wife, his daughter and his son were away from home; now the dog, his only companion, had left him, too. The son was the one who found a solution and, after qualifying as a doctor, he told its story to Dr Rhine. The dog was accustomed to getting its orders to round up the cows at milking time. So, seeing that it seemed determined to settle at Washington College, he took it outside and gave the familiar call, which he repeated several times. Old Taylor trotted off. He went back to the farm, where he carried out his daily tasks, apparently content and no longer pining.

The point of Old Taylor's adventure, however, is that he made the hundred-mile journey to Washington College, and back again to the farm, alone, unaided and without prior knowledge of the route.

The case of Tony, a small black dog of mixed breed belonging to a family in Aurora, Illinois, is especially interesting because, after his long travels, Tony was still wearing his collar. In 1945 the family moved to East Lansing, Michigan, travelling by car. They returned the dog to his original owners and, with the usual tearful farewells to a faithful pet they had loved since he was a puppy, went on their way. The dog disappeared the day he was returned and, six weeks later, found his true master standing on a street corner in East Lansing talking to a friend.

Tony was wearing his original collar, easily distinguishable because Mr D had cut it down to size for him and made a hole in the leather with his pocket-knife. It carried a tag that the dog had been licensed to someone in a neighbouring county to the south. The collar was not the only identification. Tony had the same all-black coat, an almost invisible white line running underneath his chin, down the neck and between his front legs and, most conclusive of all, an untidily cut tail. Mr D had docked it himself and made a rather amateurish job of it. It was Tony all right! He was only a year old and had never been away from his original home.

The classic of all psi-trailing cases was fully reported and documented fifty years ago. Bobbie, a pedigree Collie with a quarter strain of Scotch sheepdog in him, was taken, at the age of two, from his home on the Pacific coast in Oregon, USA, to Wolcott, a town about 3,000 miles to the east. When the car stopped *en route* in Indiana, Bobbie left the car and disappeared. The family spent a long time hunting for him but had eventually to give up and continue on their journey. Three months later an exhausted, bedraggled Bobbie appeared on their doorstep at Oregon, with a bad scar and three missing teeth.

The author Charles Alexander was so impressed by this feat that, by prolonged and painstaking research, he pieced the whole story together from accounts of people who had noted, and at times tried to catch, this sagacious and courageous dog as it sought to find its master. Bobbie had had to cross the Rocky Mountains in mid-winter and swim turbulent and ice-laden rivers, and on one occasion he had leapt into the Missouri river to avoid capture. Of course, being a lovable animal and in obvious distress, he made many friends on the way and they tried to make him stay. But it was always impossible. He had one goal and one goal only – to find his master.

Charles Alexander placed advertisements in newspapers along the route to elicit accounts from those who had seen the dog on its journey, and even plotted the route on a map on the basis of these accounts. They were quite consistent when pieced together, and revealed the suffering and tenacity of this faithful pet. Once, in a round-up of stray dogs, he was thrown into a wire cage and driven away. The moment the cage door was opened, he flew through it and disappeared with the speed of light. The van had been going in the wrong direction for Oregon. Immediately he had orientated himself and disappeared from the sight of his pursuers.

Absolutely nothing can so far explain *how* Bobbie could accomplish this feat not merely of endurance but of orientation and homing. Along with many other such examples, it is proof that dogs possess some psychic link with their owners.

Dr J. Gaither Pratt has described how a friend of his wanted to get rid of a dog, taking it five miles away through the city of Durham, North Carolina, where, coming to a crowded and densely built part of the city, he turned the dog loose, hoping that somebody would find it and keep it. When he got home, there was the dog waiting for him. The dog's pleasure at the reunion pricked his owner's conscience, and he decided not to abandon his pet after all.

The idea that a crowded, built-up, maze-like city will confuse a dog which is trying to find its owner is quite unwarranted. Captain Trapman, in *Dogs: Man's Best Friend*, even cites the case of a dog which knew how to change trains. It happened in 1901.

Mr. Jobson, a British official stationed in Upper Egypt, had been in the habit of travelling to Cairo taking Peter, his bull terrier, with him. It was a fifteen-hour journey, in the course of which the dog made itself comfortable and did not look out of the window. When Mr Jobson was transferred to Demanhour, about three hours' journey on the opposite side of Cairo, he made a journey to Cairo, leaving Peter behind.

What transpired sounds like fiction but was confirmed at the time by enquiry. Peter boarded a train to Cairo. He reached

Cairo, changed platforms, changed trains and visited his master's old haunts in Upper Egypt. Not finding him there, he entrained again for Cairo, got out there, visited several of Mr Jobson's friends, then, showing visible disappointment at not finding his master, entrained again and went to his new home at Demanhour, where he was obviously delighted to see his master had returned.

As this peregrination involved a three-hour wait at Cairo, one might well wonder where he got his sense of timing.

Trapman quotes the case of an Irish soldier who joined up in World War I, in 1914. His wife, with their dog, went to live in Hammersmith, London. Her husband was with the earliest contingents to reach France and was soon in the fighting, but after a while he was allowed weekend leave from the trenches to pay a brief visit to his family. When he returned to the battlefield, his dog refused all food and was utterly disconsolate. Then the dog disappeared. Wondering how she could break this terrible news to her husband, she waited for ten days, during which time she made desperate efforts to trace the dog. At last she wrote to him to say that their pet had vanished.

Her astonishment may be imagined when she heard from him that their dog had joined him in the trenches at Armentières, which were all the time under a heavy barrage of shell-fire. Somehow the dog had made its way through the maze of London streets (quite unfamiliar to him), traversed seventy miles of unknown countryside, crossed the Channel and, after a sixty-mile journey on French soil, 'smelt his master out amongst an army of half a million Englishmen and this despite the fact that the last mile or so of intervening ground was reeking with bursting shells, many of them charged with tear-gas!' His name was Prince, a title he surely deserved.

Another dog undismayed by a maze of streets was Boby, belonging to a florist at La Ferté-Alais, who accompanied his master to the flower market in Paris and got lost. His master and his family searched hard and long for him, without success. Five days later Boby, muddied and sore, limped home. Certainly the journey was only thirty-five miles, but the route would have puzzled a human being, let alone a dog which had never covered it.

These examples cannot be written off as mere instinct. To attach labels to puzzles does not solve them. Even to describe something as 'psi-trailing' explains nothing; nor would 'ESP-trailing'. What instinct could tell a dog which train to catch or how long to wait at Cairo station? How does a dog know that his master has gone to work in some place he has never visited? Obviously some unknown sense tells the dog what to do and where to go.

It is too commonly assumed that animals cannot *reason*. Yet many actions by animals imply logical processes of thought.

I do not mean to imply that dogs should be credited with more ESP than other animals. Frequent reference to them is inevitable because they are one of the principal classes of domesticated animals, nearer to us and under closer observation than others.

Can dogs think and reason? Dr William McDougall, who worked at one time with Dr J. B. Rhine, says in his *Outline of Psychology*: 'Most of the behaviour of animals is initiated and guided by perception, that is to say, by appreciation of impressions made on the sense organs.'

It will be noted that, even as long ago as 1923, when this classic was first published, he did not say *'all of the behaviour . . .'* Dr McDougall was aware of the existence of psychic faculties, painstaking and precise though all his research work was. I do not think he would aver today, as he did then, that, 'Of any animals lower in the mental scale than apes it is difficult to point to behaviour that clearly implies reasoning.' The cases of psi-trailing which I have quoted, even presupposing some psychic faculty which leads the dog on to the right place, also imply some form of reasoning, as, for example, that the dog knew which train to catch and which to wait for. In that instance memory played a part but could not wholly account for what transpired.

Indeed, Dr McDougall disproved his own assertions by an experiment he conducted with his own Airedale terrier. The dog had never been trained to tackle mechanical problems but, when confronted with a cubical wooden box whose lid could be opened only by pressure on a handle, soon learned how to do it – having first noted, of course, that Dr McDougall had put a biscuit inside the box.

Compared with the tricks that circus dogs are taught, and the many human situations in which dogs have behaved with great sagacity, it is difficult to maintain that dogs cannot reason. Their interpretation of situations is often far more intelligent than that of their masters.

A typical example of this is related by Williams in *Dogs and Their Ways*, published in 1860. (Lest the reader should be puzzled or exasperated by the omission of Williams' forenames or initials, I should mention that, for some reason, they do not appear on the book itself.)

A French merchant set out on horseback, accompanied by his dog, to collect some money due to him. He tied the bag containing it before him, while his dog frisked about the horse, barked and jumped, as if he too was specially joyous. After riding some miles, the merchant dismounted to rest in the shade, laying his money by him under the hedge. On his remounting the dog followed, crying, barking and howling, and, at length, began to bite the heels of the horse.

Thinking that his dog had gone mad and considering his suspicion confirmed when the animal would not drink when crossing a brook, he decided to kill the animal but feared that he could be seriously injured in the attempt. He therefore shot at the dog – not, unfortunately, with sufficient accuracy to kill him instantly. Wounded, whining and in a welter of blood, the dog still tried to crawl towards its master. Grieved and sickened by the spectacle, he rode on, feeling that he would rather have lost his money than his dog, his faithful companion for so many years.

Rather have lost his money . . . the train of thought made him glance to where it should have been. It was gone! Turning his horse, he galloped back, to find his dying pet had dragged himself to the hedge where the merchant had laid his money and was still guarding it. He wagged his tail with pleasure at seeing his master, licked his hand and then died. He had tried to tell his master, in the only way he could, that the money was left behind. His behaviour was not merely instinctive. it implied some ability to reason. Why, otherwise, bother to guard the money, when his master's strange behaviour suggested that he was indifferent to it?

Since ancient times stories of 'learned dogs' have come down to us. Plutarch wrote of a dog called Coliseum, in Rome, which had learned to be a superb actor and was a tremendous attraction with spectators, being put through his tricks before the Emperor Vespasian. The dog could perform any kind of dance and could feign illness and death and many other states. Such tricks may, of course, be taught by training, on the 'carrot-and-stick' principle. But the acquisition of learning demands some co-ordination of mental processes as well as memory.

Williams gives numerous examples of dogs trained to count and answer simple questions by motions of their paws or by a particular number of barks. A music-lover in Darmstadt, Germany, taught his pet to become a music critic, although the skill was painfully acquired. Everyone in his household had to play some instrument and understand and read music; in order that the dog, too, might play his part, he gave him a resounding whack with his cane every time a player sounded a false note. (All this was long before the researches of Professor Pavlov of the USSR into the reflex actions of animals, and brain research.) Not surprisingly, the German's dog became accustomed to howl whenever a wrong note was played and even did so *before* the cane descended. Thus the players had automatic warning that they were playing incorrectly. It is interesting that the dog learned to howl with pain *before* the cane descended; in the unusual circumstances, it was quite a sensible thing to do!

In 1949 Professor Bechterev of the USSR reported on his work with a fox terrier, Pikki, a circus dog owned by V. L. Durov. Pikki was able to carry out quite complicated tasks. Telepathy, it was thought, might be the medium between owner and dog, even though Dourov used a special whistle, inaudible to humans but audible to dogs, or made certain minor gestures which the dog had learned had a special meaning. Even minor variations of facial expressions can constitute a signal to a dog.

Bechterev tested a dog called Lord, which barked answers to

addition or subtraction problems and could indicate letters of the alphabet by a system of simple coding, based on the numerical sequence of the letters in the alphabet – one bark for 'A', seven for 'G', and so on. Bechterev did not rule out the possibility of some unidentifiable faculty at work (*psi*, as we would put it in modern parapsychological terminology), because satisfactory results were achieved usually when the experimenter concentrated. Some element of telepathy could not be ruled out, but, since we do not know how a dog's brain works, we cannot rule out the possibility of the dog *reasoning* as well. This reasoning, however, seems often to ensue from an unusual, or psychical, rapport with its master.

Dr Nandor Fodor reported in 1936 that Dr Max Muller of Munich had investigated the cases of two 'talking dogs of Weimar'. One of them, a dachshund named Kurwenal, 'barked out the alphabet according to a code'.

Just before World War II, an Airedale terrier, Lola, belonging to Fräulein Kinderman of Mannheim, was shown tapping out long and complicated answers on a code based on the order of the letters of the alphabet. It had taken Lola's owner many hard months to familiarize the dog with the entire alphabet. Mathematical queries were answered by the dog tapping with her left paw for tens and her right paw for units. She was even reported to have forecast the weather, told the time and temperature and predicted, with perfect accuracy, the number of whelps in the litter she was to deliver days later!

The significant thing about Lola, however, was that her ability to answer questions tailed off to mediocrity after an initial series of spot-on answers. This scarcely substantiated the assertions of sceptics who maintained that the dog's answers were responses to cues from her owner. If this were so, why should they tail off? Did Lola merely get bored? Since the sort of activity in which she was being encouraged is alien to a dog's normal life, this could well have been the case, but a psychologist who tested Lola for ESP (Dr William Mackenzie) put forward a quite different theory. He maintained that the tests indicated a special and unidentifiable type of mediumistic rapport, a kind of 'psychic automatism' as he put it, or, again in his own words, 'a very particular psychic relationship between the animal and its master'.

An even more remarkable case of a 'psychic' dog achieving greater-than-chance success in answering questions was the subject of a detailed scientific investigation in the 1950s. Word had got around in the USA that the Parapsychology Laboratory at Duke University was investigating the psychic propensities of animals. Mr G. N. Wood, of Warwick, Rhode Island, had been quoted in the Press to the effect that his pet dog, Chris, performed amazing feats, and news cuttings describing them were sent to the laboratory as a matter of interest. On one occasion Chris, nicknamed 'the wonder dog' as he hit the Press, indicated the correct score and some other correct details about a baseball game that had just been played – but no one present knew the outcome of that game at the time that the dog gave the answers.

Investigations proved that the performance of Chris did not depend on the picking up of cues. He would spell out answers with his paw, but the closest observation of his owner, Mr Wood, revealed no trace of a cue. Dr J. Gaither Pratt and Dr Remi J. Cadoret paid several visits to the dog and his owner in Rhode Island and found, with controlled tests, that in 500 trials with ESP cards Chris could exceed the laws of chance to an incredible degree.

In one set of tests, packs of twenty-five Zener cards, as used in telepathy experiments, were shuffled at Duke University and put into numbered boxes. These were then posted. The 'agent' would cut a pack of cards and then observe them one by one, until he had worked his way through the pack. In another room the dog Chris and his owner Mr Wood were out of sight and hearing of the 'agent'. Chris had been taught to tap with his paw from one to five to indicate the different symbols on the cards – once for a circle, twice for a cross, three times for wavy lines, four for a square and five times for a star. At one time Chris astounded everybody by scoring *a hundred per cent success*!

There was absolutely no possibility of Mr Wood's knowing what cards were likely to be turned up. At Duke University the randomized order of each pack had been recorded, and although the agent in the experiment would cut (not shuffle) the pack, any attempt to tamper with the pack would have been detected by comparing the new sequence of cards with the original. The process of cutting the pack would merely split one series of symbols into two series. Chris gave his answers by pawing the arm of Mr Wood and, later, Miss Rosemary Goulding who collaborated in the experiments. With the latter eleven runs (a run being going through a whole pack of twenty-five cards comprised of five different symbols) produced 104 successful answers. The normal average of correct guesses would be one in five. In eleven runs the score should be fifty-five. According to the laws of chance, a score of 104 in eleven runs could happen only once in 100,000 million such series – odds of 100,000 million against! No chance explanation could account for the dog's feat.

4

Dogs – Friends of Man

In man, true friendship I long strove to find,
but missed my aim;
At length I found it in my dog most kind.
Man! blush for shame.

This tribute to his dog, inscribed on a silver collar, was written by a Mr Henry Hawkes of Halling, Kent, over a century ago. He was returning late from Maidstone market and had celebrated so liberally at Aylesford that he left the inn quite drunk. The countryside was covered with thick snow and there was an intense frost. He staggered and fell about, nearly drowned while passing the river at high water and at last, able to go no further, rolled on his back and fell asleep. His dog scratched the snow about him, climbed onto his master's chest and lay there all night, undoubtedly saving him from dying of exposure.

As dawn broke, a neighbour called Finch passed that way with a gun and heard the dog bark. As he approached, the dog made every sign of welcoming him, getting off his master's body and shaking the snow from his rough fur. Hawkes was very near death, both his heartbeat and his pulse being very feeble.

Wordsworth wrote a lengthy and touching tribute to another dog which, starving and distressed though it was, refused to leave the body of his master. As Mr Charles Gough of Manchester, accompanied only by his dog, tried to cross one of the passes at Helvellyn in the Lake District, he lost his way in the gathering darkness and fell into a deep recess. It was a remote spot, and many weeks passed before the dog's faint barking was heard at last and the tragedy discovered. Wordsworth finished his poem in this way:

> Yes, proof was plain, that since that day
> When this ill-fated traveller died,
> The dog had watched about the spot,
> Or by his master's side.
>
> How nourished here through such long time
> HE knows, who gave that love sublime;
> And gave that strength of feeling great
> Above all human estimate.

The strength of a dog's devotion is so often proved that one is bound to ask, as dog-lovers have asked for centuries, how and why it is that this extraordinary bond should exist between man and dog. Not only are dogs known for their loyalty: they show the sort of courage which in a soldier would earn the Victoria Cross. There exists, in fact, an award for dogs who distinguish themselves in exceptional danger – the Dickin Medal, which is awarded by the National Canine Defence League.

The case of Rex, a black-and-white collie, is typical. He was owned before the Second World War by a family in Ferriby, east Yorkshire, and was especially fond of his mistress's grandchild, three-year-old Roland.

Like most small boys, Roland loved adventure and at three was too young to understand the hazards. Having often seen grown-ups cross the road, he gave his parents the slip one day and did it himself. Soon he was crossing a busy main road. Lorries braked frantically as he appeared unexpectedly from in front of a moving vehicle, and drivers swerved dangerously to avoid him. The lad reached the point where he was in obvious danger whatever he did. He could neither retreat nor advance in safety. Rex, seeing his predicament, watched for gaps in the traffic, then edged him towards the pavement.

It was not the only time Rex saved Roland's life. A few weeks later Roland wandered into a brickworks and, seeing a brick pond, waded in to test its depth. It was deeper than his own height, and he began to sink and to panic. Rex, following him, dragged him to the bank.

Roland's next adventure was assumed by his sad parents and the villagers, who mustered all their numbers to search for him, to be his last. One evening he disappeared and, as evening fell, nearly fifty villagers, using torches and lanterns, went looking for him on the waterfront of the Humber. It was feared he had slipped into the icy waters and drowned.

By dawn hope had almost been abandoned when a farmer's wife thought she heard a baby's cry. Going to the farmhouse window, she saw a little figure with a dog pushing it towards the farm. Rex had done it again. It transpired that the dog, finding the child on the river bank, had led him, in the gathering dusk, to the comparative safety of the meadows. It was a bitterly cold night, in which Roland could well have died from exposure, but the dog's warmth saved him. At dawn the child had wandered off again, the dog only just edging him away from a main railway line along which express trains tore at top speed, and thence to Humberside Farm.

Swansea docks once boasted an aged black retriever who saved not one but *twenty-five* people from drowning. 'Swansea Jack', as the dog was affectionately known by everyone, would patrol the quays and, at the first sound of a splash and a cry, would be swimming to the rescue. This was in the 'hungry thirties' when many were unemployed and all manner of tests (including the Means Test) were applied before an unemployed man could claim the dole. Some conditions were very harsh: one chairman of a magistrates' bench, Sir Frederick Senier, even declared that an unemployed man could not afford to keep a dog. In those days a dog licence cost a mere two pence a week, and dog biscuits – hard, firm biscuits enriched with meat meal and bone – could be bought for a few pence. However, if Jack's owner had found himself out of work, Jack would have been either given away or destroyed.

Not merely the heroism but the intelligence displayed by dogs is impressive. Many years ago Mrs Clarke, a platelayer's wife, was walking along the railway at Backworth in Northumberland when a strange dog seized her coat and pulled her with such determination that at first she thought it was attacking her. Looking down, however, she noticed that, in gripping her coat, the dog had dropped a child's shoe from its mouth. The dog no sooner saw her looking down at the shoe than he picked it up

again and rushed ahead. She followed the dog, which led her to
three infants who had strayed onto the railway line.

It was not a minute too soon, for none of them was more than
three years old, and all were oblivious of the danger. She picked
up one small boy and took him clear of the line. Meanwhile, two
tiny girls had clambered off the rails onto the track just as a train
approached with belching clouds of smoke so dense that it is
improbable that the driver would have seen the children. When
the train had passed, Mrs Clarke found that a shoe of one of the
girls had become jammed between a fishplate and a bolt. Evidently the other two children had been trying to release their
playmate. The dog had seen the danger and gone for help, with
the child's other shoe in its mouth.

In the Victorian magazine *All The Year Round* is a description
of the intelligence displayed by a dog that looked after a blind
man: 'There is a dog resident in the Borough of Southwark who
keeps a blind man. He may be seen most days in Oxford Street,
hauling the man away on expeditions wholly uncontemplated by,
and unintelligible to the man; wholly of the dog's conception
and execution. Contrariwise, when the man has projects, the dog
will sit down in a crowded thoroughfare and meditate. I saw him
yesterday wearing the money-tray, like an easy collar, instead of
offering it to the public, taking the man against his will . . . to
visit a dog at Harrow.'

In Victorian times a blind beggar and his dog were a popular
sight in Dean's Yard, Westminster (by the Abbey). The Westminster scholars used to like to lean out of the windows and
throw halfpennies, which the dog would carefully collect and
take to his master. Sometimes they amused themselves by hiding
the coin in the mud, but the dog invariably retrieved it.

A writer of this period, Mr Ray, describes a blind beggar in
Rome whose dog was so intelligent that, the moment his master
called for alms at a house, he would lie down. When the talking
stopped and money had changed hands, he would rise of his
own accord and proceed to the next likely house, avoiding the
residences of the non-givers and pausing where alms had been
given before. Sometimes people would throw food from the
windows, which he would retrieve, but he would not touch a

crumb of it until he had given it to his master and received from his master's own hands any that could be spared. The spectacle of devotion and intelligence delighted the people of Rome, who maintained that the dog had never been trained to its task but merely 'took to it'.

Although we know little of the inner workings of a dog's mind, nobody would dispute that dogs are as capable of emotion as are human beings. Anger, hate, courage, suspicion, joy and heroism, not to mention loyalty and devotion, are all manifested in different but discernible ways. Joseph Taylor, in a work published in 1804, mentions an instance which he considered conveyed a mixture of anger and grief.

A member of Parliament maintained a pack of foxhounds which were all in hot pursuit of one bitch. The bitch produced a litter of puppies, which, like their mother, were allowed to roam about the house. However, their owner decided that the puppies were not worth raising, as they were partly mongrel. So one day he took the puppies, while the mother was taken out for a walk, and drowned them in an ornamental lake in the grounds.

There was no apparent reason why the bitch should have had any idea of what had happened to her puppies, or who had caused it to happen, but the occurrence had a strange sequel. On returning to the house, she totally ignored her master and rejected any friendly advances. The following day, when taken for her customary run in the grounds, she plunged into the ornamental pond and, fiercely resisting all attempts to drag her out, drowned there in full sight of her master. He was shaken by the experience, feeling convinced that the dog had discovered his guilt and had no desire to live after the death of her offspring.

Can dogs *reason*? Many veterinaries and writers who have made a close study of dogs have concluded that they do. In a book called *Dog Stars*, the wife of T. P. O'Connor, an editor influential before the First World War, describes how she took her dog, Max, to a veterinary surgeon for treatment to an injured leg. Months later, Max met a mongrel limping with a damaged paw and, Mrs O'Connor tells us, led it to his vet, whom he trusted to mend the mongrel's leg too.

There are many authenticated stories of dog-to-dog loyalty.

All of them suggest a reasoning process. Memory would not in itself account for what happened. Memory could account for Mrs O'Connor's dog's recognizing the vet who had treated him but could scarcely account for his behaviour in taking *another* dog to see him!

Captain A. H. Trapman, author of *The Dog*, attributes reasoning power to a dog belonging to an old lady from Salford in Lancashire. She had been in failing health for some time, and from time to time had to lie down on her bed and send for the doctor. But on two occasions she had visited the doctor's surgery, accompanied by her dog.

One day, when the servants were out, a telegram was delivered telling her that her son had been killed in action in France. She flung herself upon the bed, sobbing with grief, while her dog sprang up and tried to comfort her. Finding that it failed to sooth her, it tried frantically to find a way out of the house, eventually nosed a window open wide enough to get out and trotted along to the doctor. The doctor, noting the animal's distress, allowed himself to be led back to the house.

Captain Trapman interprets this incident as follows: 'When mistress lies on the bed in daytime the doctor is sent for. All the servants are out, therefore I must go to the doctor, since mistress is lying on her bed.'

In 1804 *The Spectator* opened its pages to readers' accounts of canine intelligence. One of the most striking concerns a man from Aberdeen who was crossing the frozen surface of the River Dee when the ice broke. The pieces around him were each insufficient to take his weight; as fast as he seized one, it broke in his hands. His plight was desperate. His dog watched this drama for about two minutes, then disappeared and returned with a wooden pole, long enough for the man to rest upon two of the larger pieces, which he could hold on to until help came. Then the dog raced off to the nearest house and barked and yelped until help was forthcoming, leading the rescuers to the spot.

The loyalty which dogs demonstrate towards their owners they often feel for each other. A close affinity often ties dogs, and when one is in distress the other often shows considerable sagacity in coping with a wholly unexpected situation. An instance of this occurred in Cornwall just before the Second World War.

A spaniel on a visit to Harrow-Barrow, near Callington, with its owner, Mr W. T. Pooley of Browning Road, Devonport, chummed up with a local dog. The two would gambol and chase each other at breakneck speed near an old mine-shaft which had not been used for over thirty years.

Suddenly the spaniel fell in. Its playmate scampered off home, whining to attract the attention of neighbours, who followed it to the head of the mine-shaft, where the whines of the trapped and injured dog could clearly be heard. Mr Guest volunteered to do down and found that the dog had, by a lucky chance, landed on a ledge a hundred feet down and, although slightly injured, was not much the worse for its experience. For his act of bravery in rescuing this dog in distress, as a result of the warning brought by its loyal and intelligent playmate, Mr Guest was awarded the silver medal of the National Canine Defence League.

Williams, in *Dogs and Their Ways*, describes how a dog 'took pity' on a cat being stoned by some young ruffians in Liverpool. They were dragging it through a dirty pond when the dog, distressed at the sight, set upon them one by one, sent them on their way and then rescued the bleeding cat from the pond and bore it to his own quarters. The dog even brought it food, and the sight of the cat-and-dog friendship was one of the main attractions for many years at the Talbot Inn.

The same author relates how two dogs, inseparable companions, set off from London to Devonport on what proved to be a mission of revenge. Their master had previously taken one of them with him on a business visit to the same town, where it was attacked by a watchdog. The mauled and injured dog, on returning to London with his master, went absent with his canine friend – a sturdy, very large house-dog – and was missing for ten days. Later their master received a letter from the owner of the watchdog to say that the two dogs had visited his home and killed the dog that gave the first offence.

Apart from the remarkable fact of enlisting the help of his companion to come with him on the journey and 'sort out' the offending watchdog, it is clear that the dog which made the first journey to Devonport with his master led his companion unerringly to the correct house, in the right street and in the right town. He had been taken by rail, yet found the way on foot.

In a previous book, *Ghosts and Hauntings*, I gave many instances of ghostly animals being seen and of animals reacting violently to scenes of alleged hauntings. Similar cases are constantly coming to light, but not all have a sinister connotation. Both in the past and in the very recent present there have been cases reported where the 'ghost' of a dog, for instance, has shown a protective concern for the living.

One classic case of a dead dog seeming to help his master dates back to the American Civil War. When a man called John Simpson, serving in the Federal Army, was found asleep under a haystack with a black-and-tan mongrel, the soldiers who found him searched his pockets and discovered papers proving that he belonged to the Confederates. He was a spy – although, it would seem, an extremely amateurish one.

Simpson was hauled before Colonel Panton, the commanding officer, and after summary questioning was sentenced to be shot at 8 a.m. the following day. He showed no signs of fear on hearing his sentence but asked that his dog might be with him during his last night of life. The Colonel refused and, after the prisoner was led away, gave orders for the dog to be killed at once. The dog was then beaten to death with rifle butts.

In the morning, as the condemned man was led to his doom, he asked where his dog was and his escort, wishing to avoid the embarrassment of telling him the truth – or perhaps wanting to get the whole thing over without histrionics or fuss – lied to him, saying that his pet was being well looked after. 'That's good,' Simpson replied, 'though he ain't much good to look at, he is far and away the best buddy I've ever had. Promise, boys, that you'll look after him.'

The four soldiers promised and took up their positions as a firing squad, pinioning their prisoner while Colonel Panton waited to give the command to shoot. As they tied him up, the condemned man looked down at a point just in front of his feet and said, 'Why, it's Pete! I knew the old fellow would come to say goodbye if he possibly could.' 'He's gone nuts.' said one soldier irritably, and hastily blindfolded him. The firing squad then awaited the word of command to shoot, but noticed that Panton had gone deathly white; he was staring at the same spot just ahead of the condemned man. Three times he opened his mouth to give the command. No sound came. At last, visibly shaken, he muttered 'execution deferred' and walked away.

That same night the Confederates attacked and in the fighting Colonel Panton was killed. Simpson was released by his fellow officers. Simpson maintained to the end of his life that Pete had come back from the other world to be with his master in his greatest danger, and in so doing saved his life.

A more recent example of the ghost of a dog being of service to human beings was reported in 1980, when Stella Sellors, of Belper, Derbyshire, and her husband were hopelessly lost on a Cornish moor. When they saw an animal exactly like an aunt's dog which had once led her to safety when she got lost on a Yorkshire moor, instinctively she said, 'Hello, pet.' The dog went ahead, leading them for two miles to the top of a path leading to the beach they had hoped to find – then disappeared behind rocks.

An amazing story of a dog that appeared to have psychic sense in the generally accepted meaning of the word came to light in 1985, when Pero, a sheepdog belonging to Mrs Gwen Pugh of Portmadoc, South Wales, went missing. Mrs Pugh suspected that the black-and-white dog must have sneaked aboard a de- livery lorry that had called at their farm earlier in the day and, on telephoning the lorry owners, found that this was indeed so. Pero was now 120 miles away.

It was arranged that Pero would be handed back at a halfway rendezvous but the following morning the lorry driver rang to say that Pero had gone missing again. It was a great blow to Mrs Pugh and her family for they loved their ten-year-old pet. Appeals through the police and the RSPCA, even an appeal on the local radio, produced no clue.

A week later Mrs Pugh's daughter, Mrs Sian Evans, who was on holiday at her in-laws' home in Burry Port, south of Carmarthen, phoned to say, 'Pero is here with me.'

This was almost incredible. Burry Port is fifteen miles south of Carmarthen and in the opposite direction. The sheepdog had turned up on the doorstep of Mrs Evans' holiday home, having never been in that town and having never visited that house. How Pero knew where to find the house is an utter mystery. Now Pero the peripatetic sheepdog is back on the farm.

5

A Flash of Strange Light

'There is in every animal's eye a dim image and a gleam of humanity,
a flash of strange light, through which their life looks at and up to
our great mystery of command over them, and claims the fellowship
of the creature, if not of the soul.'

John Ruskin

Ruskin wrote those words nearly a century before the world
awoke, belatedly and in a mild panic, to a realization that
every species is interrelated in Nature, and that mankind is
not something separate from and, as so arrogantly postulated,
superior to the rest of creation. He not only wrote but *felt*, with
the insight of a poet and a mystic, that ignorance about animals,
cruelty to them and unthinking exploitation of them demean and
impoverish man himself. Any harm to animals, or indeed any
ill-treatment or persecution of any species of living thing, even
insects or birds, does more, probably, than merely upset the
balance of nature. Animals have their psyches, like human beings.
There is ample evidence of individual consciousness in all of
them. They hunt for food, copulate, breed, nurture and protect
their young, build their homes, co-operate with each other, and
form social systems and elaborate rituals concerned with such
things as mating and asserting their right to territory. They have
means of communication with each other – sometimes, as with
birds, silent and instantaneous, like a flight of starlings on the
wing and flying in a particular direction, in formation, by some
mysterious signal.

Animals have brains. Whether animals (and other living creatures) have 'minds' or 'souls' is admittedly unproven – but

scientists and others have not even agreed on whether these exist in human beings either, or even on the definition. Argument continues on whether the brain is a kind of super-computer, its functions mechanistic and physical, or if it operates under the supervision of an 'unseen overseer' called the mind. And the question of whether death constitutes transition or oblivion puzzles all who are not committed to some doctrinal and dogmatic assertion as an integral part of some adopted faith; it is a question which has not yet been answered scientifically, even though many scientists of distinction from Faraday to Sir Oliver Lodge, or from J. W Dunne (*Experiment with Time*) to Sir Aleister Hardy, have asserted their faith in survival.

By 'psyche' I mean the individuality, the unique something which comprises you and distinguishes you from every other human being who has existed since the world began, from every other human being in the world today, and from every other human being yet to be born.

Personality, individuality, the soul, the psyche – whatever word one uses, it refers to the uniqueness of each human being. We all have something in common with each other; equally, we all have something special to ourselves.

This being true of ourselves, on what grounds do we assume a monopoly of it? If the human being has a soul, why should a dog, not less useful, free of many of the vices and defects to which humans are prone, not have a soul also? Or the cat? Or the ape? Or the elephant? If anything survives of human personality, if the Spiritualists are right in their assertion that a 'spirit world' exists, then why should it be 'inhabited' (if that is the word) by semblances, forms or vestigial survivals of former human beings *only*? Spiritualists, of course, maintain that animals do 'survive' in the spirit world. The concept is difficult to grasp, since they live (as we do) in a physical environment, in a balanced ecology, dependent directly or indirectly upon one another. The apes need their jungle, the birds their trees and bushes, the fish their waters.

How, I wonder, could such a balance be maintained in a non-material existence? There are philosophical snags in the hypothesis, too. As to the survival in another world of the forms of life that exist on this, where would the line be drawn? Why should a dog enjoy another existence, if a rodent did not? What of viruses and disease-bearing germs?

Whatever the merits of these speculations, there is absolutely no doubt that the dog, surely man's oldest friend and certainly one of the most useful and devoted, has an extraordinary affinity with human beings and possesses gifts and abilities which are as mysterious as they are impressive. As anybody who has ever possessed a dog knows, each is a distinct personality. There is much evidence of psychic propensities. Dogs have been known to respond to telepathic signals. Their orientation is a mystifying business – they have made long and dangerous journeys across completely unknown territory, finding the place or the master they sought. Phantasms of dogs have been frequently seen, in every country and century, suggesting that *something* of the dog's psyche can survive, even if the visual image received by a human being is a kind of 'imprint' left behind by the once-living creature.

Not only are dogs seen as ghosts, but dogs have been known to behave as though they have seen ghosts, and to exhibit fear and terror in allegedly haunted places. They are very much affected by psychic phenomena.

As with cats, dogs have been known to demonstrate the gift of precognition, seeming to be aware of impending calamities, either by way of natural disaster, man-made accidents or destructiveness, or of the death or illness of their masters. They exhibit a high intelligence and an ability to reason. We are inclined to dismiss anything unexplained about animal behaviour by ascribing to it the word 'instinct', which may explain some things but by no means all. Professor MacDougall, the eminent psychologist, declared himself 'staggered' by the intelligence manifested by the common earthworm, which, in drawing a leaf inwards to block the entrance to its burrow, seems able to perform mathematical calculations as to the angles involved and the best manner in which to achieve its purpose. Yet the worm has no brain, despite giving clear evidence, as MacDougall saw it, of reasoned intelligence in tackling a problem.

At what point in history did man and dog become the inseparable companions they are today? In his *Natural History*, Georges Buffon (1707-88) considered that the shepherd's dog was the original of the 'whole race' – meaning, I suppose, the first of a rapidly expanding range of breeds. Thus he describes the shepherd's dog as 'the root of the tree'. But from the standpoint of natural history, this assumption may seem arbitrary or incapable of proof. A more modern view is that the dog became domesticated in stages, first as a camp-follower, then as a semi-nomad, hanging about camps becoming more familiarized with men and more docile in their company because of frequent visits, and finally, by virture of mutual dependence, accepting man as companion and friend.

The most generally held theory amongst dog experts is that the dog is descended from the wolf. Zoologists are not so sure, pointing out that everywhere the eye of the dog has a circular pupil, while the position or form of the pupil is oblique in the wolf. However, a Mr H. C. Brooke, of Welling, Kent, in the last century, succeeded in making a wolf his friend and companion. It was trained to follow him and showed submission and affection. When Mr Brooke went away for a long period, and the wolf was relegated to a menagerie, he pined for his master and for a long time refused food. The occasion of his master's return aroused one of those frantic demonstrations of sheer joy of the sort one would have expected from a completely domesticated animal. He had not seen his master for eighteen months and had become friendly with his keepers, yet the moment he heard his master's voice again his recognition was instantaneous.

The experience was repeated: his master had once more to leave on a protracted absence, returning to a warmer welcome than ever. For the rest of the wolf's life, he was his master's devoted companion, thus proving that there is not much difference between wolf and dog when it comes to befriending man.

In archaeological terms, the ruins and relics discovered by archaeologists do not necessarily tell the whole story. Thus, the fact that skeletons of dogs have been found dating back to neolithic times (from about 7000 BC), in settings that show they were domesticated and part of a household, does not prove that they did not fulfil a similar role earlier, perhaps even much earlier. The discovery of dog skeletons in kitchen middens in Denmark, dating back to this period, tells us something of the roles of dogs in that period. We know, too, that the early Stone Age dwellers of Britain kept dogs as pets or companions over 7,000 years before Christ.

To describe the dog as 'man's best friend' may be a well-worn cliché, but its constant use is based upon truth. It would be impossible to record, or even begin to record, the immeasurable debt that man owes to dogs. But the conception of this debt is devalued if we do not accept that the dog's devotion and service derive not from a slavish or timid compliance but from a sense of affinity and a high intelligence which are in many ways superior to our own. The dog's instincts are subtle and not easily explained; in modern terms we would say that dogs have ESP or psi – faculties beyond explanation. This was well understood in the ancient world, where dogs inspired not merely gratitude for service and devotion but awe and respect.

That ancient Egypt should have worshipped dogs can probably be explained by the fact that the rising and falling of the Nile, on which the irrigation of the land, and therefore the very survival of the people, depended, was heralded by the appearance of the star Sirius, the Dog Star. This was the signal to abandon the lower plains to the flooding of the fertilizing waters and to remove the flocks to higher ground. Just as the dogs protected the *fellahin* and their sheep, so did Sirius save them from starvation. They associated the prompt appearance of the star, which coincided with the revitalizing flooding of the land, with the fidelity of their dogs.

In Ethiopia (formerly Abyssinia) the people not only worshipped dogs but elected a dog as their king. The animal was maintained in magnificent state, surrounded by guards and officers. Its behaviour and reactions were 'translated' as responses to reports and requests. If the dog fawned and wagged its tail, this was interpreted as an expression of royal pleasure. When it growled, it was assumed to disapprove of the way the country was being governed. Its edicts, as interpreted by courtiers and priests, were promptly fulfilled. The dog barking or showing his teeth to a visitor or servant was tantamount to a death sentence.

The dog cult in Egypt influenced Pythagoras of Samos, who travelled throughout the East and Middle East in search of knowledge. He returned convinced of the reality of reincarnation, maintaining that at death the soul entered the body of an animal. But of all animals, Pythagoras considered the dog pre-eminent, and he would hold a dog to the mouth of a dying man to receive his departing spirit, in the belief that no animal could better perpetuate its virtues.

Buffon, who describes so well the feelings of man towards his dogs, thought as did Pythagoras:

> The dog, independently of his beauty, vivacity, strength and swiftness, has all the interior qualities which can attract he regard of man. The tame dog comes to lay at his master's feet his courage, strength and talents, and waits his orders to use them; he consults, interrogates and beseeches; the glance of his eye is sufficient; he understands the signs of his will. Without the vices of man, he has all the ardour of sentiment; and, what is more, he has fidelity and constancy in his affections; no ambition, no interest, no desire of revenge, no fear but that of displeasing him; he is all zeal, all warmth and all obedience; more sensible in the memory of benefits than wrongs, he soon forgets, or only remembers them to make his attachment the stronger.

This 'attachment' is so extreme and so moving that it deserves our close attention. It suggests a psyche orientated to its master – a unit, in effect, of two separate types of consciousness. The rapport is frequently so strong and so remarkable in its manifestations that it presupposes some *psychic* force, some element we can neither define satisfactorily nor comprehend. Generalizations about 'instinct' or 'dogs have been domesticated for centuries' do not even begin to account for the stories of heroism, intelligence and loyalty to man which have characterized dogs since recorded history began.

Amidst the ruins of Pompeii, destroyed by the eruption of Vesuvius, followed by an earthquake, on the night of 24 August AD 79, was found – long afterwards – the skeleton of a dog stretched over that of a child. The manner in which they lay permitted the assumption that the dog had laid himself over the little child to protect him from the lethal hot ash that rained down on the city. Further investigation showed this to be so. A dog collar was found by it; its fine craftsmanship indicated that the dog must have been something special. The inscription on the collar stated that the dog's name was Delta, that his owner was a man called Severinus, whose life the dog had saved on three occasions. Once he had dragged his drowning master from the sea; he had driven off four robbers during an ambush; in a grove sacred to the goddess Diana, near Herculaneum, he had saved his master from an attack by a she-wolf. Such, until the volcanic eruption and earthquake, had been Delta's proud record, which had been capped by this final act of heroism. For Delta was devoted to the master's little boy (and would allow nobody else to feed him). How one can visualize that dramatic scene! Delta did not fly for his life in terror; his only concern was for the little child he loved and tried vainly to save.

We may well ask what is this rapport between dogs and humans, so strong that it surpasses the natural instinct for survival, alleged so often to be the strongest and most ineradicable of all instincts? Again and again one sees that a dog accepts a human being as master or mistress, thereafter subordinating its instinct for survival to its sense of duty and devotion. 'Uneasy sleeps the head that wears a crown' is more than a saying; it is a historic fact. Many a ruler has escaped assassination because his dog could be trusted when no human being could be. Andronicus, Emperor of Constantinople in the twelfth century, had reached that eminence by so much killing, violence and intrigue that he dared not depend on his own bodyguard to protect him while he slept. He relied on a great Albanian hound so fiercely protective and alert that nobody dared go near the Emperor's chamber.

From earliest times monarchs and leaders have felt themselves strengthened by the company of a dog. The ancient Egyptians knew well the debt that they owed to their dogs and commemorated their devotion by many a statue. Cheops, in whose reign nearly 4,000 years before Christ, the great pyramid of Ghizeh was commenced, had a favourite hound, Abakaru, as his constant companion.

Alexander the Great, who tested his dog's courage with such opponents as a boar and a bear, found his dog would be content with no adversary less than a lion, which it attacked with such ferocity that the two animals were only separated with difficulty. Though it sounds apocryphal, that same dog, Perites, fought and defeated an elephant! Small wonder then that Alexander the Great (who had distinguished himself in battle at the age of sixteen and was king at twenty) slept soundly with Perites at his side! Small wonder, too, that when his beloved pet and companion died, Alexander named a city after him.

The whole world can desert a man, but nothing can ever destroy the psychic bond uniting a dog and its master. About the middle of the last century, Williams, who wrote *Dogs and Their Ways*, described how, during the French Revolution, just before the overthrow of Robespierre, a tribunal condemned 'an upright magistrate and most estimable man' on a fabricated charge of conspiracy. When he was seized, his spaniel was with him and fought hard to accompany his master, whose pitiless captors at first refused to allow him even this meagre consolation in his misery. So the dog took refuge in a neighbour's house, returning every day to the prison door, always at the same hour. For a long time he was refused admittance, but his devotion eventually won over the porter, who allowed the dog to enter, and, as Williams puts it, 'Joyful was the meeting that took place.' To the last sad moment the dog refused to desert its master: 'The gaoler, however, fearful for himself, carried the dog out of the prison, but the faithful creature returned the next morning, and was afterwards daily admitted. When the day of the sentence arrived, the dog, notwithstanding the guards, penetrated into the hall, where he crouched beneath the legs of his master. Again, at the hour of execution, he was there, and when the guillotine had done its horrid work, he would not leave the headless corpse.'

The kindly neighbour who gave the dog refuge found that he disappeared night after night. Search revealed him stretched on his master's grave. Every morning without fail the dog would return to the grave, 'accepting food from its protector's hand'.

Eventually, however, even this sustenance was refused, and for twenty-four hours a day the dog lay where his master was buried, and was seen, in his weakened state, trying to dig up with his paws the earth that separated them. There he died.

It is said that Sulpicius, a powerful and wealthy Roman who incurred the displeasure of his emperor, was deserted by everyone, even his family and friends, when he was deprived of his honours and wealth. Everyone, that is, except his dog. The dog would not desert him, following him into prison despite every effort to frighten him away, and appearing at his master's execution. At the moment of beheading the dog went almost mad with rage, fighting the executioner until he too was killed by the sword.

In modern times, there was the Skye terrier who loved his master, Auld Jock, so dearly that when the poor shepherd died in 1858 he would not leave his grave in Greyfriars churchyard, Edinburgh. The little dog endeared himself to everyone, but neither the proffered food nor the games he would occasionally play with young children would take him away from his master. Every night, without a single exception, in heat, in cold, in rain, snow or blustery winds, Bobby returned to the grave. When he died after fourteen years of devotion, a fountain with his statue on its was erected in his memory. Edinburgh has many statues, but this fountain commemorating the memory of Greyfriars Bobby, the faithful terrier who watched over his master's grave until his own death many years later, is still a loved and revered landmark, esteemed more highly than statues erected to the famous.

Over a century ago the *Liverpool Mercury* reported a similar tale of dogged devotion:

A dog in this town visits all the newspaper offices every day. He generally honours our establishment with his first visit. For some hour or hour and a half, he reclines on the flags of one side of the doorway, eyeing the passers-by and each person who enters. Then he rises, and proceeds to the next adjoining office, the *Standard*, where, having gone through the same observance, he repairs to the *Mercury*, and again renews his apparent penance. Thence he goes to *The Albion, The Journal* and *The Times*, at each of which places he similarly spends about the same space of time, which completes his daily gyrations. It is surmised that he is the dog of some defunct newsman.

Napoleon, whose military adventures caused and enabled him to witness scenes of indescribable cruelty and bloodshed before he ended in exile on the island of St Helena, was moved to tears by the devotion of a dog. In 1796, in the course of his Italian campaign, as he took a stroll through the battlefield, in 'the deep silence of the night', as Napoleon put it, a dog, leaping suddenly from the body of its dead master, rushed upon Napoleon, then returned to its hiding place, howling piteously. Alternatively he licked his master's hand and rushed towards Napoleon.

Napoleon recorded the tremendous impression made upon him by this unbreakable link between dog and master: 'No incident on any field of battle ever produced so deep an impression on me. I involuntarily stopped to contemplate the scene. This man, thought I, had friends in the camp, or in his company; and now he lies forsaken by all except his dog! What a lesson nature here presents through the medium of an animal!'

6

The Inexplicable Cat

Stately, kindly, lordly friend,
Condescend
Here to sit by me.
    'To a Cat', Algernon Swinburne (1837-1909)

The poet Swinburne expressed in a few words what cat-lovers have observed for thousands of years: that the cat is inscrutable, yet admirable. It is not so demonstrative in its affections as a dog. It seems in many ways detached, as if possessing secrets it does not intend to share, even with the most loving mistress or master. It seems to *know* things, to a degree sometimes puzzling, on other occasions quite staggering. Can cats read thoughts? Can they sense where their owners are, even miles away, in totally unfamiliar territory? By what mysterious instinct do cats trek through strange places and succeed in finding their owners or returning to their original homes?

When the cat was befriended and domesticated by man, as in ancient Egypt, it handsomely repaid the debt (if debt there were). Often cats were used as food-tasters. If a cat turned away from a dish the food was assumed to be poisoned and thrown away. No doubt some lives were saved by these means, but probably sometimes unjustified accusations were made against suspects, since cats might well reject food acceptable to humans but disagreeable to them. More importantly, cats kept down the numbers of rats and mice, which not only caused famine by their destruction of crops but might well have been suspected, though medicine was then in its infancy, of causing disease and plagues. But it was not, as we know, the merely practical value of cats which earned them respect, love and often actual worship; it was the appreciation of the wisdom and special insight which they were observed to possess. The Prophet Mohammed is reputed to have cut off the sleeve of his coat to avoid disturbing his sleeping cat. He did not do this because his cat was a good mouser but because he saw in it a creature worthy of the greatest respect and gentle treatment. For the same reason Queen Marie Leczinska, wife of King Louis XV of France, decreed that cats should have the freedom of the city. Woe betide any French citizen seen to ill-treat a cat!

Cats are nocturnal creatures, and this perhaps accounts for the feeling that they have some secret world of their own. Their eyes sometimes gleam in the dark, like lamps, and this, too, accounts to some degree for their varying reputation as either deity or devil. That cats often see *something* invisible to humans is obvious to anyone who has owned a cat and observed its behaviour habitually. The cat's head turns, and its eyes follow with lively interest something which others cannot see at all; it seems to be watching an invisible presence, often in such a manner as to suggest that the presence, whatever it may be, is passing, approaching or even moving up and down stairs. Cats often react as though being stroked or fondled by unseen hands, or show fear of some presence they sense as hostile.

Many famous people have owned and loved cats, and cats have been the friends of many writers and men of letters – the poet Gray, Dr Johnson, Charles Dickens and the Brontës among others. Dr Johnson was a noted cat-lover: for Hodge – the last of a long line of pets – he went out each day to buy oysters, then admittedly a relatively cheap food. But according to Boswell, he took on this chore 'lest the servants having that trouble should take a dislike to the poor creature'. Boswell tells us further that the Doctor was careful of Hodge's feelings. One day, as the cat sat purring in his master's large lap, Boswell praised it, observing that it was a fine cat. 'Why, yes,' said Dr Johnson, 'but I have had cats I liked better than this.' Then, 'as if perceiving Hodge to be out of countenance', he added, 'But it is a very fine cat, a very fine cat indeed.'

In lighter mood, Johnson's near contemporary, Thomas Gray, wrote an epitaph to Selima, a cat who died attempting to raid the goldfish bowl. In our day, T. S. Eliot produced *Old Possum's Book of Practical Cats*; the American wit, Don Marquis, created Mehitabel, the office cat who believed she was the reincarnation of Queen Cleopatra and, in the watches of the night, condescended to recount her Egyptian adventures to Archie, the cockroach. On the other hand, Napoleon could not bear the sight of a cat.

Perhaps people with a power complex feel that the cat, with its suggestion of superior wisdom and aloofness, represents some sort of threat to their dominance.

Cats in Britain have been domesticated for about a thousand years, and certainly when they were first introduced they were valued as livestock and found worthy of protection; indeed, Hywel Dda ap Cadell (Howell the Good), a Welsh prince of the tenth century (d. 950) famous for his code of laws, included the most severe punishments for anyone found killing or injuring a cat. Hywel, of course, was concerned with the cat's merits as a mouser rather than as a companion, still less as a companion with any mystical attributes. The story of Dick Whittington, the poor boy who came to London in the reign of Edward III, accompanied by his cat, and who, leaving the city despondent at his bad luck, was persuaded by the ringing of the bells to return and make his fortune, becoming Lord Mayor of London, is historically true. It is also true that he was as devoted to his cat as to any human companion, and there is good reason to think that he attributed much of his good fortune to it.

The late Vita Sackville-West, in a delightful and erudite monograph on nursery rhymes, remarks on the 'curious persistence' of the cat in the stories of all nations, and the remarkable similarity of the word for 'cat' in different and widely separate languages – i.e. *cattus* in Latin, *katta* in Byzantine Greek, *katt* in Saracenic, *katti* in Finnish, *cath* in Welsh and Cornish, 'and just plain *cat* in Gaelic'.

So far as the origins of cats in Britain are concerned, they are thought to have been brought from Egypt via Cyprus, so that they are in direct line with the sleek cats of ancient Egypt to which temples were erected.

The Middle Ages, with their dark superstitions and religious

persecutions and tyranny, were as unlucky for cats as for human
beings. The witch mania resulted in thousands of faithful pets
being burned along with the supposed witches. As we have seen,
the idea gained ground that the Devil disguised himself as a
black cat; from the supposition that any old crone who muttered
to herself or talked to her cat was in league with the Devil, it
was but a brief transition to the assertion that, in talking to her
cat, she had been talking to the Devil.

At the annual Festival of St John in France, cats were thrown
into a bonfire.

It is highly probable that, the cat population being so widely
and senselessly reduced, the mouse and rat population, freed of
its natural predators, increased tremendously, as did the diseases
they carried. The fearful Great Plague of London (1664-5),
which claimed over 100,000 lives in a single year, was a rat-borne
plague. The odious habit of sacrificing cats, sometimes as a
supposed precaution against fire in a building, is recalled by a
gruesome exhibit in the local museum at Cricksea, Sussex: the
mummified body of a cat and her kittens found plastered into a
cottage wall.

As a pleasant contrast to all this cruel ignorance, actors and
seamen were invariably kind to cats, which they regarded as
lucky. Even today the black cat is a symbol of luck – the exact
opposite of the medieval belief.

There is, as I have asserted with some detail in my book *Ghosts
and Hauntings*, an immense amount of factual evidence that what
we term 'ghosts' are seen, heard and sometimes even felt.
Poltergeist activities are reported to have created havoc and
terror from ancient to modern times and, whatever the explanation, there are innumerable authenticated accounts of such
happenings. In reply to the question of whether human personality survives, or whether apparitions are some kind of living
presence as distinct from a subjective hallucination, I can only
state my own belief that emotion and mental energy are not
necessarily as transient as they are too easily assumed to be. I
have never accepted that either emotion or thought disappears
as soon as it has been subjectively experienced. On the contrary,

I hold that in circumstances we do not at present understand, and by processes not yet fully investigated, emotion leaves its imprint on so-called 'inanimate' things – objects, places or buildings – and that it is these impressions which certain sensitives can pick up.

If human identity survives in any form, I see no reason to deny that the same may hold good for animals. Surely one cannot assume the survival of some creatures and not of others? Where could the line be drawn between those species that survive and those which do not? If the lovable cat lives in 'the beyond', will the sparrows be there too, for the cat to catch? Would heaven include the natural enemies of man (though they are not necessarily without their use in the whole balanced, complicated ecology) such as the tsetse fly, the staphylococcus or the python?

If my premise that thoughts and emotions leave a permanent and reproducible impression upon places and objects is a valid one, animal 'ghosts' would be seen as well as phantoms of human beings. Indeed, they have been. Ghosts of cats are seen frequently not merely by human beings but by other cats – and other animals.

One of the most terrifying and best authenticated of ghostly cats is the Black Cat of Killakee, accounts of which go back to the eighteenth century. This 'demon cat' sounds a really terrifying spectacle. It was seen fairly recently by Tom McAssey, an Irish artist, whose portrait of the apparition now hangs in Killakee Art Centre, in the Dublin mountains. The Dower House, a long white building which was once the home of the Massey family, titled landowners with huge estates in those parts, was said to be haunted not only by 'ordinary' spectres but also by the ghost of a very large cat.

This is not surprising, if one accepts that terror or sickening cruelty may leave some impression on the surroundings. A few hundred yards away, on Montpelier Hill, all manner of evil was perpetrated by the Irish equivalent of the Hell Fire Club, where Black Masses were said. One local legend tells how a local 'buck', Thomas Whaley, caught a farmer's daughter in a gin-trap like a wild animal, killed her, smoked her like a side of bacon and shared out the cadaver between his equally degenerate friends. Another recounts the killing of a deformed youth, who was tortured to death for 'fun'. Evidence of this was found in the course of building alterations in 1968, when a skeleton was discovered having small bones and a disproportionately large skull. It is probably because of the house's evil associations that William Butler Yeats joined in ceremonies at the Dower House: the poet had been initiated into the Hermetic Order of the Golden Dawn, of which the notorious Aleister Crowley was a member. Such ceremonies could include the ritual killing of a cat. However, the Killakee cat was seen and written about 200 years before black magicians came upon the scene.

Tom McAssey's encounter with the Killakee cat was described in the *Dublin Evening Herald* in December 1968:

> On a dark evening of March of this year I was painting in the gallery when one of the two men with me remarked that the door in the old stone hall had opened. Half an hour earlier these men had seen me locking the door and pushing a six-inch bolt into its socket.
>
> We stared for seconds into the darkening hall-way. Then I felt compelled to go to the outer door. A shadowy figure stood there. For a moment I thought someone was playing a trick. I said: 'Come in; I see you.' A low guttural voice answered: 'You can't see me. Leave this door open.'
>
> The men standing directly behind me heard the voice, but thought it spoke in a foreign language. They ran. A long-drawn snore came from the shadow. In a panic I slammed the heavy door. Halfway across the gallery I looked back. The door was open again and a *monstrous black cat crouched in the hall, its red-flecked amber eyes fixed on me.*
>
> I went directly to my room and painted the animal exactly as I had seen it. The picture hangs there as mute evidence of that visit. Several times afterwards the black monster was seen by different people, until a clergyman came and, standing at the big door, read the prayer of exorcism.

A rather uneasy place, one would have thought, in which to run an arts centre but, under the able direction of Margaret O'Brien – who is clearly not a nervous type, it enjoys vigorous life.

A novelist who was always seeking background for colourful

thrillers, F. W. Gumley, heard of the Massey Estate and its brooding, derelict house in the early 1930s and decided to make his own exploration of it in search of ideas. The friend who suggested to him that this might be a rewarding exercise did not exaggerate.

Mr Gumley decided to pay his visit at nightfall, travelling by car, sensibly enough accompanied by two friends. He took a torch with him. They drove up a lonely mountain road and finally stopped at a small lodge:

> We entered the gate, I was going ahead with the torch, and entered a narrow pathway bordered with trees and bushes with the old mansion looming somewhere ahead. I had only gone a few paces when I called out a warning to those behind: 'Look out! There's a dog ahead!'
>
> It had seemed to me that a black animal the size of a cocker had crossed the path a couple of feet ahead of me at right angles and gone soundlessly into the bushes ahead. We hung back for a moment, expecting perhaps that the dog would attack us, for after all we had no right to be there at all. However, nothing happened. I was very intrigued by this incident as I had heard that the old house was haunted, and I made quite a number of visits after nightfall, invariably accompanied by a friend. About ten o'clock one winter's night, my friend and I were about to cross over the wall when we saw in the moonlight the gleaming eyes of a large cat confronting us. We got quite a start . . .

In the 1920s, contributors to the *Daily News* of London had some remarkable stories to tell of ghostly cats:

> We once owned a small black cat that was as devoted to us as any dog could be. Unfortunately, it contracted some disease, and had to be painlessly destroyed by the chemist. But the little wraith came back to the home she had so much loved. I saw here where she liked to be best, playing by the bannisters on the landing, near our bedroom, where she used to come and have breakfast with us every morning. A visitor to the house saw her frolicking with a doormat in a way she loved to do; and a maid met her on the stairs.
>
> I never have known a more intelligent little cat, nor one that loved her home and owners more, so it was of great interest to find that after death she came back in that way.

An encounter with a ghostly cat in a convent – its whereabouts, unhappily, not specified – was described by another reader. She was staying at the convent where, according to tradition, the west corridor was haunted by a grey cat. Being very fond of cats, she decided to investigate and went down the corridor (a lonely subway under the road) at midnight:

> It was rather a wild night, and great gusts of wind made the windows and doors creak as I descended. The place was dimly lit by gas jets always burning. To my surprise – and I think awe – I was just entering the corridor when I saw the figure of a grey cat comfortably seated in the middle of the path before me. I approached it, for all fear went at the sight of the beautiful animal. That it was alive I was certain. I stopped and lifted the creature into my arms. I put the cat out of a little window on the ground floor and turned and descended the stairs.
>
> I turned to looked back into the gloomy corridor once more. Below me, on the last step, and looking up with large, staring eyes, was a grey cat. I was so certain that I had locked and barred the little window that I could not understand this. I felt an uncanny feeling that this really was a ghost. I fled.
>
> Next day, I went over the place inch by inch to see if there was any way the cat could have got out. On talking to a nun about my experience, she smiled and said: 'That was the night Sister Aileen died. It was a favourite cat of hers. It never comes back any other time.'

In the twenties a family, having lost a much-loved cat called Tommy, found almost immediately that a stray cat appeared on the scene. It soon made itself at home and enjoyed sharing tea with them. But before settling into the armchair once used by its predecessor, there was always a lot of scuffling, as though it had first to cope with an invisible foe. Ears back, it would snarl and spit and lift its paws in attack or defence but then, after about twenty minutes of this behaviour, would take up a position in the chair and settle down to sleep. This strange rubric was a delight to the children of the household, who saw nothing sinister in it. The cat, had, incidentally, been named 'Bolo' after a French spy whose trial in Paris was creating a sensation.

In ancient Egypt cats were revered and worshipped as goddesses. Hundreds of thousands were mummified, and so highly regarded was the cat that to kill it was a capital offence. This is the Gayer-Anderson cat, around whose neck is the Eye of Horus or Utchat

The monument in Edinburgh to Greyfriars Bobby, a Skye terrier which loved his master so dearly that on his death he stayed at his graveside for fourteen years, until he himself died

Jack the baboon operated the signals on the railway at Uitenhage, South Africa for a number of years at the end of the last century. His master, the signalman, was crippled in a train accident, so Jack took over the operation of the levers, seldom making a mistake

This monument in Freiburg, West Germany commemorates a duck which saved thousands of lives by quacking loudly throughout the town before a devastating air raid by the RAF. But for its warning, many more thousands would have died in the heavy bombing that followed

Heidi, a dachshund-terrier cross, was a highly intelligent dog which forewarned danger and seemed to know when its owner's mother was about to die

Guide dogs are highly trained to provide invaluable assistance to their blind owners. The close bond between dog and owner is one of the best examples of human-animal rapport

Quadriplegic Sue Strong, who is almost totally incapable of movement, with Henrietta, the Capuchin monkey which is her constant companion and help. Henrietta opens bottles, mixes drinks, picks up books for Sue to read and then brings her the 'mouth stick' with which she turns the pages. This understanding animal saves Sue Strong from total dependence upon other humans

Five minutes before the IRA bomb went off outside Harrods o 17 December 1983, Queenie the police dog sensed that something was wrong and tried to drag her handler, PC John Gordon, away from the scene. Queenie had to b destroyed as a result of her injuries, but she succeeded in saving her master's life

This monument stands outside Shibuya station in Tokyo, Japan, commemorating a dog named Hachiko which met his owner off the same train every day for man years

Adele Lithman and Bob Holborn, deep sea diver, sport with a friendly dolphin named Percy off the coast of Cornwall

Although there have been fatal accidents in John Aspinall's zoo, he himself has a most unusual rapport with wild animals. In this picture a tigress is even letting him handle one of her cubs!

Bolo's ghostly encounter is by no means the only instance of its kind. Paule V. Hampso of Bucks describes in *The Cat-Lover's Journal* of 1974-5 an almost exactly similar experience:

A few weeks previously, we had lost our dear cat, Dina under the wheels of a car . . . and her loss upset me dreadfully. She was part of the family, but I decided that I would again open my door to another feline creature, and we purchased two adorable Brown Burmese which we named Aquarius and Scorpio.

Dina's original basket was in use again – and it was placed, as always, just by the radiator in the lounge. At that particular time, my sister and brother-in-law were visiting us, and it must have been around the 10 p.m. mark when suddenly, Aquarius' and Scorpio's hackles were raised several inches! They appeared to be staring at the basket. Their backs were arched – they were spitting, and I immediately thought that each had offended the other in some way. They went on for some four or five minutes . . .

Given the evening's performance, I said to my husband, after our guests had left, that I hoped our pets would not offend each other too often. He replied quietly that he had seen Dina sitting in her basket quite happily, gazing round the room and finally staring at him, at which point she faded out as noiselessly as she had come. I asked why on earth he hadn't said anything at the time, to which he replied that it would only have upset me – which was true.

Although some cat ghosts, especially the legendary ones, *are* frightening, one does not often hear of such apparitions attacking their former owners. One correspondent of the *Daily News*, however, related how a pet cat was destroyed 'wantonly' for the purely selfish reason that its owner was going on holiday and could not be bothered to make provision in her absence for her pet's care. Shortly after the owner returned from holiday, a friend who visited her noticed that on several occasions she jumped up in alarm, saying that the cat was back and had scratched her leg. Once a long, scratch-like weal appeared on her leg after such an incident. These disturbances became so chronic and were so alarming that the woman had the house exorcised and was not troubled again.

Sylvia Barbanell, poet and widow of the late Maurice Bar-

banell, editor of the *Psychic News*, is, as was her husband, a
Spiritualist. She believes that the spirits of animals go on living
and claims to have seen the 'ghost' of a favourite cat, Snoopy,
fleetingly and in shadowy form, in their flat.

A hair-raising story of a ghostly cat in the Old Manor House,
Oxenby, was related by the late Elliott O'Donnell in *Animal
Ghosts*. The story was well corroborated by witnesses and was
related to him by a Mrs Hartnoll, a Classics teacher in an
exclusive preparatory school in Clifton.

Mrs Hartnoll had been brought up as a child in the Old
Manor House, Oxenby, which dated back to the reign of Edward
VI and had some distinctly unprepossessing features. It was grim,
faced with split flints and edged and buttressed in cut grey stone.
To the centre of its gloomy front was the device of a cat,
constructed out of black shingles, with white shingles for eyes.
In the moonlight, the effect was certainly spooky.

The house itself was rambling and fantastic, with a great hall,
gallery and windows of stained glass embodying all manner of
strange motifs and designs, some decidedly mystical or esoteric,
such as squares, triangles, witches, dragons and cats. There were
two towers, completely circular within and, according to Mrs
Hartnoll, 'half included in the building' which contained the
winding staircases of the mansion leading to the upper floors. If
a storm were raging, the luckless guest or resident, ascending to
their apartments, could almost feel as if they were borne aloft
on an angry tempest, so great was the noise as the wind thundered
against the windows and casements.

There was one corridor, low and vaulted and enclosed, it
seemed, in an unnatural silence. On more than one occasion
Mrs Hartnoll felt a tangible menace there, a feeling that something was waiting to pounce out at her. Once she heard a loud,
clanging noise, followed by the sound of rushing footsteps, and
felt something tearing past her, a shadowy form whose nearness
left her completely paralysed. Terrified, she fainted on the
spot.

On another occasion, near the same spot, she heard sounds
of a 'furious scuffle' and, on looking up, saw staring down from
the balustrade the ashen-white face of a very evil-looking man

with long, narrow features. His mouth was cruel and thin-lipped. Her immediate reaction was to flee in terror, but curiosity brought her back to the spot and, stealing to the foot of the staircase, she looked up:

> Just as I was passing one of the doors, it opened. I stopped – terrified. What could it be? Bit by bit, inch by inch, I watched the gap slowly widen. At last, just as I felt I must either go mad or die, something appeared – and, to my astonishment, it was a big, black cat! Limping painfully, it came towards me with a curious, gliding motion, and I perceived with a thrill of horror that it had been very cruelly maltreated. One of its eyes looked as if it had been gouged out – its ears were lacerated, whilst the paw of one of its hind legs had been either torn or hacked off. As I drew back from it, it made a feeble and pathetic attempt to reach me and rub against my legs, as is the way with cats, but in so doing it fell down, and uttering a half-purr, half-gurgle, vanished – seeming to sink through the hard, oak boards.

For over a century now, the Society for Psychical Research has been recording and assessing reports of ghostly animals. In 1884 a mother and daughter, Mrs Griefenberg and Mrs Erni-Griefenberg, were having their 'mid-day dinner' when both saw a large white Angora cat with green eyes under the table. The cat marched round the table, went noiselessly out of the door and, half-way down a passage, turned, stared at the two women and then 'dissolved away' under their eyes. The same thing happened a year later in Leipzig. The two women signed a statement describing their experience, which was filed with the Society in 1890. Then there was the case of a pure-bred blue Persian called Smoky, which occurred on 12 July 1909. Smoky was owned by a lady whose identity was known to the Society but who was shielded by the anonymity of H. L. 'Green'.

> July 12, 1909. My sister H. L. 'Green' had a favourite cat called Smoky, a pure-bred Persian of a peculiar shade, and small. There was no other cat in the village the least like her.
> In the spring she became ill, and died about the middle of June, 1909. The gardener buried her, and planted a dahlia over her grave. Shortly before Smoky died she had been worried by a dog, and had her ribs broken, so that she walked quite lame. This injury was the final cause of her death.

On July 6th, 1909, my sister and I were at breakfast, and I was reading a letter aloud to her. I was sitting with my back to the window, which was on my sister's left. Suddenly I saw her looking absolutely scared, and gazing out of the window. I said 'What is the matter?' and she said 'There's *Smoky*, walking across the grass! We both rushed to the window and saw Smoky, looking very ill, her coat rough and staring, and walking lamely across the grass in front of the window, three or four yards from it. My sister called her, and she took no notice. She ran out after her, calling her. I remained at the window and saw the cat turn down a path leading to the end of the garden. My sister ran after her, still calling, but to her surprise, Smoky did not turn or take any notice, and she lost sight of her among the shrubs.

About ten minutes afterwards, my sister and a friend living with us saw Smoky again, going through a hedge in front of the window. My sister again went out after her but could not find her.

She was next seen about half an hour afterwards by the servant in the kitchen passage. She ran to get her some milk and followed her with it, but the cat walked away and from that moment disappeared completely. We made every enquiry of the neighbours, but no one had seen her, or any cat like her. Of course we thought there had been some mistake about her death, though our friend, the gardener and the boy had all seen her dead. The gardener was so indignant at the supposition that he had not buried the cat that he went to the grave, took up the plants and dug up the body of Smoky.

We are quite mystified at the occurrence, which was witnessed by four people, namely: Mr B. J. Green, H. L. Green, Miss Smith and Kathleen B. (Servant). When last seen, the cat was walking towards —— House, next door, but when my sister went over there, the people knew nothing of her. When my sister *first* ran out after her, the cat *ran* away in front of her, moving fast, but on one side, as she did before she died . . .

A story current in Germany years ago, when many people lived whose parents had related it to them, concerns the ghost of a cat that kept appearing to frighten the man that drowned it.

There lived in the Odenwald an old woman who used her cottage window to display a few humble items for sale, an assortment such as the 'diddymen' used to bring to the doors of British homes in Victorian days – cheap pipes, buttons, thread, inexpensive cotton prints and so on. Her sole companion for most of her life was the cat, which was never away from her. Eventually the old woman married a young sergeant – almost young enough to be her grandson – who was interested only in her money. When she died in 1869, Sergeant Lautenschlager, as his name was, wanted to clear the house. But the cat would not leave its mistress, keeping ceaseless vigil by her body, so that Lautenschlager, out of patience, seized it roughly and drowned it in the River Mumling nearby, where it runs close to the edge of the road between Michelstadt and Steinbach.

When he remarried (quickly), his new wife found he frequently arrived home frightened and exhausted, complaining that, as he passed the river at that spot, the ghost of the cat he had drowned ran alongside him. When he married a third time, his wife heard from his lips the same story. One wonders why, in the circumstances, he did not take another route; but perhaps there was not another he could take.

7
Cats:
Their Secret Wisdom

That cats have a secret wisdom of their own, and some kind of prescience that puzzles and impresses, is common knowledge to all who care about cats and observe them closely. Their ways are sometimes strange indeed, as attested by the gipsy-linguist and author George Borrow, who tells the story of an ecumenical cat.

In 1854 Borrow, accompanied by his wife and daughter, decided to tour Wales. They chose Llangollen as their centre and took lodgings there in a house which had once been the vicarage. One afternoon, as they sat at dinner (well into the Victorian era, 'dinner', the main meal of the day, was taken between 3 p.m. and 5 p.m., earlier in the country and, more fashionably, later in town), a black cat slunk in. It was a wretched creature, emaciated and suffering from some skin disease, as well as innumerable wounds. The kindly Borrow at once fed it bread and milk, which the half-starved animal took up greedily. The next day it re-appeared at the dinner hour. This time the Borrows' landlady happened to be in the room. As soon as she saw the cat, she started to shoo it away roughly but she was stopped by Borrow, who insisted that the cat should be left alone. The landlady retired in a huff; the cat was fed and was soon curled up asleep.

Borrow was puzzled by the cat's condition, which seemed the result of an unusual hostility on the part of the usually placid population of Llangollen. He soon pieced the story together. It seemed that the black cat had belonged to the Church of England vicar when he occupied the premises the Borrows were now renting. But he had moved on, leaving the cat behind. Now the inhabitants of Llangollen were Dissenters to a man and seemed to think, as Borrow put it, that the vicar's cat was tainted by Church of England doctrine. So they took it out on the poor animal, harassing it, pelting it with stones and rubbish, chasing it away from any refuge where it tried to sleep. The landlady of the vicarage was its most determined enemy, and the cat soon learned to avoid the premises at all costs. Later an English family, whose members belonged to the Anglican Church, took up residence in the cat's old home, and despite its previous unhappy experiences in that place, it seemed to know it would now be safe there. But how did it *know* that? Why did it come back? Could it know that it was the victim of religious persecution?

In its domesticated state, the cat is a friend of man, but, like tigers and lions, larger and more spectacular members of the family, it is also a predatory animal. Yet naturalists have noticed outstanding exceptions to this rule – instances of cats striking up a friendship with mice or even suckling puppies, the young of a class of animals they normally avoid. Such examples are a reminder that nobody really knows how a cat's mind works, how it interprets what it sees, just how much it observes. Gilbert White, in his *Natural History of Selbourne* (1789), gives two examples of strange attachments:

My friend had a little helpless leveret brought to him which the servants fed with milk in a spoon, and about the same time his cat kittened and the young were despatched and buried. The hare was soon lost, and supposed to have gone the way of most foundlings, to be killed by some dog or cat. However, in about a fortnight, as the master was sitting in his garden in the dusk of the evening, he observed his cat, with tail erect, trotting towards him, and calling with short, inward notes of complacency, such as they use towards their kittens, and something gamboling after, which proved to be the leveret which the cat had supported with her milk, and continued to support with great affection. Thus was a germinivorous animal nurtured by a carnivorous and predaceous one!

Why so cruel and sanguinary beast as a cat . . . should be affected with any tenderness towards an animal which is its natural prey, is not so easy to determine.

In the same work, White mentions a cat suckling three young squirrels 'with the same assiduity and affection, as if they were her own offspring'. 'This circumstance,' he comments, 'corroborates my suspicion that the mention of exposed and deserted children being nurtured by female beasts of prey who had lost their young, may not be so improbable an incident as many have supposed; and there may therefore be a justification of those authors who have gravely mentioned what some have deemed to be a wild and improbable story.'

White's observations remind us that even so 'wild and improbable a story' as Edgar Rice Burroughs' *Tarzan of the Apes*, written long afterwards, had some nucleus of inherent probability, even though the author (who was surprised at its instant and worldwide success) had done his best to think up the most bizarre and unlikely human quandary his imagination could devise.

There are two fields of ESP where cats appear to have superior and unexplained knowledge: orientation (as when a cat finds it way to places it has never been to) and precognition (foreknowledge of events to come).

In the latter category, cats have often helped their owners (and still do), to escape from danger in the nick of time. Their thoughts have not been primarily for themselves; although their instinct for survival is so strong, they have thought for their owner's safety first. Dr Ute Pleimes, a German psychiatrist working at Giessen University, has collected over 800 cases of pets warning their owners of impending disaster, and a high proportion of these concern cats. 'I have seen enough,' she says, 'to convince me that animals do have a special psychic power to sense danger before it happens. We are fools to ignore them.'

A woman living in Malvern told a *Sunday People* reporter in 1974 of a rather unnerving experience: 'When my husband lay ill our cat never left his side, but one day she leapt from the bed with her hair standing on end. She lashed in the air with her naked claws as if fighting off an invisible intruder. In horror I turned to my husband and was just in time to take him in my arms as he died.' It will be recalled that Winston Churchill's cat behaved in somewhat similar fashion immediately before his death. It had previously refused to leave his bed, but on the day he died it left the house a few hours beforehand, as though it knew the end was near.

That cats can act protectively has long been observed. In *The Law of Psychic Phenomena* (1922) by J. J. Hudson the story is related of 'a gentleman in India'. He recalled: 'I was lolling on the sofa drowsily reading a newspaper when Tom came in and began to mew most plaintively. I waved him off, but he came back again, varying the mews with signs of an offensive attack, his coat bristling and his tail waving. On looking under the sofa on which I had been lying, I discovered a cobra in the act of springing. My gun being handy, I shot the cobra. You should have seen Tom's satisfaction; he ran between my legs, rubbing himself against them as if to say "Well done, Master".'

The lives of three families were saved by a warning from their cat some years ago in Balham, London. A fire had broken out on the ground floor. At three o'clock in the morning, when everyone was asleep, one woman lodger was awakened by a kitten scratching at her bedroom door. When she opened the door, she found the passage in flames. There was just time – and only just – to warn her hosts, and the families on the top floor and in the basement. The lives of ten people were saved in that incident although, sadly, the kitten that gave the alarm died in the flames.

The exploits of cats which are determined to rejoin their friends or owners are still a mystery to scientists. Sooty, a cat belonging to Mr and Mrs T. Henthorn of Newbury, walked nearly sixty-five miles to their former home in Wolverton in Buckinghamshire. It took eleven weeks to do the journey. Then its owners received a telegram informing them that Sooty had arrived at her old home, tired and bedraggled.

That appears to be a case of a cat more attached to its home than its owners, but the reverse is often the case. The owner of a pet shop in London's Camden Town once recalled the case of a woman customer who bought a cat from him and lived with it in her house in nearby Regent's Park. After a while she decided to move to a flat in Brighton, Sussex – a flat she had never been to before. In the course of the move the cat got lost, yet by some instinct of its own it turned up at her flat days later! Since the cat had never been to Brighton, still less to that flat, how did it know where to find her?

Beverley Nichols, the novelist, once had a black Persian cat which he gave to a friend, Mrs Ronald Haylock, who took it with her when she moved from Saffron Walden to Hempstead, Essex. But the cat missed its best friend, a dog, and padded off in search of it. The cat made the seven miles journey. It had never been far from Saffron Walden but arrived at last in a sadly dishevelled state, to greet its old pal, Pan, the house dog, with affection and relief.

What is sometimes called the homing instinct in cats, and what the late Dr J. B. Rhine (who, with a team, did research into similar cases two decades ago) called 'psi-trailing', was the subject of an enquiry in 1940 by the *News Chronicle*. The paper reported the astonishing feat of Peter, a Siamese cat that walked 180 miles from Ashburton in Devonshire to its home in Surbiton, now virtually a suburb of London.

The persistence and courage of cats on these long treks are impressive. The same newspaper reported how a cat made its way through the New Forest *three times* in order to transport its kittens. The cat and its litter were given away and taken 2½ miles miles across a lonely stretch of the forest. 'Four days afterwards,' Mrs A. Hiscock, of Southampton, reported, 'the cat and the kittens were on the back doorstep. The cat must have walked the distance three times, carrying the kittens in relays.'

An even more spectacular example of 'psi-trailing' and caring for its young at the same time was recorded in the case of an Irish cat. A farmer on his way to Belfast with a load of hay was walking beside his horse and cart when he heard a cat mewing. He climbed to the top of the load and found a cat and three kittens settled comfortably in the hay. The farmer transferred them to a shelter he made in the hedge, intending to pick them up on the return journey, but when he got back they had disappeared. A month later, while working in the fields, he saw the cat carrying her kittens home in her mouth, one at a time. Every hundred yards or so she stopped, put a kitten on the ground and went back for another of the family. She brought them safely back over fifteen miles, but she probably travelled about seventy-five miles by going back every hundred yards to bring them along one by one. In addition, she had to find her own food!

Like other 'psi-trailing' animals, that cat was totally unfamiliar with the territory she was traversing. How, one wonders, did she know where or in which direction to go? There were roads and fields to cross, hedges to get through, detours to make. But by some process which it seems fair to call ESP the animal persisted in its difficult and hazardous journey, certain of its directions, sure of its deviating and circuitous route.

Cats are, of course, peculiarly adapted to the requirements of survival. The phrase 'as many lives as a cat' has a certain truth in it. We talk of a cat's 'nine lives'. There is, in fact, a fairly recent case on record of a cat surviving an incredible series of mishaps. Surely the most accident-prone cat in Britain, Sam, a Siamese cat belonging to Mrs Marie Clark, of Slough, Buckinghamshire, managed to be dropped, trapped, stung, nearly drowned, crushed, roasted and hanged – and then narrowly escaped being burnt to death in a blaze!

As a kitten, Sam was dropped on the doorstep and sustained a cracked jaw. 'Concussion,' said the vet. It looked bad, but Sam recovered. He next disappeared while his owners were out visiting. His piteous mews at last located him behind a brand-new ornamental fireplace, which had to be ripped out to release him. Next he ate a bee, which stung him in revenge. His head became swollen and he could not eat for a fortnight. Next he slipped inside a laundry bag just in time to be tumbled into the washing-machine where, fortunately for him, he was spotted. He then decided to join the rubbish being ground up in a passing refuse lorry; the dustman heard his plaintive mew just before tipping the dustbin in. Next, Sam was found hanging by his collar from a tree. His eighth life was squandered when the home caught fire; he had passed out and a fireman revived him with the kiss of life!

There is nothing particularly psychic about that cat's extraordinary record, and there are very many similar cases. Probably that

is where the phrase 'a cat with nine lives' originated centuries
ago. Their capacity to survive accident after accident must have
been observed. But when it comes to cats finding their way
across enormous tracts of unknown territory and finding some
individual in a city as vast as Greater London, with its millions
of inhabitants and thousands of traffic-jammed streets, some
unknown faculty must certainly be at work. Instinct simply does
not explain the phenomena. Some link must remain between
cats and human beings, that cats can retrace their owners over
such distances and against such odds.

Years ago the parapsychology laboratory of Dr J. B. Rhine
conducted a survey of 'psi-trailing' – a description which he
applied as being appropriate to cases of pets trailing their owners
by 'psi' (psychical propensity). Over fifty dramatic cases were
investigated by the exacting and precise research standards of
Dr Rhine and his assistants. The source of any information had
to be reliable. The identity of the animal under survey had to be
established beyond all doubt, preferably by some distinguishing
mark or characteristic (for example, although cats can look
superficially alike, each, as with humans, is highly individualistic
and, indeed, unique in the permutation of its characteristics.)
Nevertheless, for research purposes, nothing can be taken for
granted. It does not follow automatically that a Blue Persian with
a slight limp that last left New York is the same limping cat that
turns up in Cincinnati. Again, some degree of corroboration is
sought. A unilateral account of an occurrence may well be
truthful but scientifically may be unacceptable; there remains
the question mark over the informant's soundness of memory,
observation or even mental health.

Dr J. Gaither Pratt, the American parapsychologist who
worked with Dr Rhine at Duke University, has related how a
member of the university staff brought a cat fifteen miles from
its home to add to the experimental colony of cats being used
for ESP tests. The cat raced off with the speed of light when its
box was opened, to appear at its home the next day!

A classic case of psi-trailing is that of Sugar, a cream-coloured
Persian which trailed its owners 1,500 miles across rugged and
difficult country. The family was moving from California to

Oklahoma, but the cat refused to get into the car which was taking his owners away. Perhaps the noise and excitement prevailing in a home about to be abandoned were the reason for the cat's flight. Some believed that the cat didn't care. However that might be, Sugar was adopted by neighbours but after sixteen days disappeared. The family were sad to leave Sugar behind. The owner, principal of a school in Anderson, California, had raised it from a kitten; owner and pet were devoted to each other.

Fourteen months later the principal's wife was in the barn of their new home in Gage, Oklahoma, standing with her back to an open window, when she felt something land on her shoulder. It was Sugar! In her surprise and fright she had, as an automatic reflex action, brushed off whatever had fallen on her. But as she saw what it was, she almost cried with joy and incredulity. A deformity of the cat's left hip joint proved beyond question that this was Sugar, the pet they had so sorrowfully left behind in California. Somehow Sugar had traversed the Great American Desert and the Rocky Mountains.

A few years ago France was much touched by the story of a cat called Mastic who, with his brother Pinceau lived in the home of a plasterer named Ligier at Luxière-les-Mines, in the Allier. One day the family moved to Sainte-Genevieve-des-Bois in the Seine-et-Oise, a distance of about 165 miles. Pinceau settled in, but Mastic disappeared after two days, finding his way home over strange territory.

France, it would seem, has more than her fair share of peripatetic cats. In 1982 a French family took their cat, Gringo, to a holiday cottage at Saint-Tropez. When they returned home, their pet went into the sulks and then suddenly vanished. Six months later he turned up at their Saint-Tropez home, having travelled 350 miles across strange territory to get there!

At about the same time the Ehmig family moved from a Paris suburb to the village of Goudargues, about 400 miles away. Blanchette, their white cat, showed signs of restiveness in her new home and took off for her old familiar home in the Paris suburb. Five months later, bedraggled and starving, she was found pawing the doors of the flat. She was seen by a neighbour, who wrote and told the family. Now Blanchette is happily settled with Mrs Ehmig's parents in Paris.

In 1983 a British cat given to an animal home by Ivan Lee of Barnstaple – who could no longer afford to keep him – got away and, a year later, turned up at his master's home. The puzzling thing is that this was a distance of a mere twelve miles, much shorter than the journeys of many cats over strange territory, and what he was doing in all that time nobody knows.

A Soviet parapsychologist, Barbara Ivanova, has decided that cats can be not only telepathic but precognitive. Describing her experiments with her own cat, Dayashka, in her Moscow home, she claims that her cat can understand what she says or even what she is thinking. Once his nose was dirty and she said, 'Your nose is dirty! Wash it!' 'I said it jokingly,' she recalls, 'but he immediately began to groom his whole nose area. How could he know what I wanted him to do?' On another occasion she told the cat to leave her alone and to play 'with your string'. Immediately the cat stopped harrassing his owner and played with his string instead.

As for thought-transference, 'Dayashka once pulled a nail out of the wall . . . when I described this to a friend in his presence he immediately ran over to the very spot and began to illustrate, by pantomime, how he had pulled out the nail!' That was too much: 'It not only suggested telepathic communication (he caught on to our thoughts or the sense of our conversation) but his behaviour suggested vanity, pride and many other human qualities . . .'

In the 1950s, experiments were carried out in the Parapsychological Laboratory at Duke University by Dr Karl Otis, and later by Dr Otis in collaboration with Mrs Esther Foster. The basis of the experiments was to give the cats the choice, in a maze, of entering one of two arms. One led to food, the other did not. The decision as to what was or was not the desirable part of the maze was entirely random on the part of the experimenters. Naturally, account was taken of the fact that the cat's nose leads it to its food; but this was obviated by a specially designed fan which blew against the food, away from the cat. Such experiments produced no particularly exciting results, but the percentage of correct choices by the cats, being higher than could be explained by chance alone, left the experimenters with the impression that some unexplained factor was involved.

One test, indeed, suggested that cats must possess some degree of clairvoyance, for it was arranged that neither of the experimenters knew which of the two arms of the maze was being selected at any given moment as that leading to food. Still the cats gained a higher-than-average score. Since they could not have picked this up telepathically from either of the experimenters, it was concluded that some degree of ESP remained.

That cats, in common with many other animals, birds and even fishes, frequently have a premonition of coming disaster, is beyond question. Earthquakes and floods in particular are often preceded by displays of distressed behaviour from cats and other domestic animals.

It may be that cats possess some special sensitivity of hearing that enables them to hear noises coming from inside the earth, some shifting of layers which the human ear cannot distinguish; perhaps they know by instinct that such noises presage disaster.

A quite different sort of foreknowledge, which would be truly described as precognition, lay behind the experience of a man who was shaving himself in the German town of Magdeburg in 1944. While he was shaving, a cat's piteous and persistent mewing made him open the front door. On the step was a stray cat he had often stroked and spoken to on the other side of the city. Local reports at the time maintained that the cat even pulled at his trousers (a very unusual thing for a cat to do) as though demanding that he leave the house immediately. Very puzzled, the man hastily dried his face and followed the cat, which kept looking back at him as though to be assured that he was really following.

After half a mile of walking the cat stopped in its tracks. Overhead came the roar of Royal Air Force Lancaster bombers. A tremendous bombing began, one of the first bombs flattening to the ground the house he had just left.

The stray cat he had befriended had saved his life.

8

Horse Sense

Horses he loved, and laughter, and the sun,
A song, wide spaces, and the open air . . .

So wrote W. Kersley Holmes in Flanders after the Battle of
Messine, of a brother officer killed in battle.

Until the invention of railways and of the internal combustion
engine, the horse was man's principal form of transport and
(windmills and watermills excepted) almost the only supplement
to Western man's muscle-power. For thousands of years the
horse was man's constant and valued companion. They lived
together. They fought together. They have been able to do this
because, as every horse-lover knows, there is a definite link,
some say a psychic link, between horses and human beings. 'I
believe that animals have been talking to human beings ever
since we were all made and put into this world . . . and I feel
that, as animals are so much quicker in picking up our thoughts
and words than we are in picking up theirs, they must have a
very poor opinion of the intelligence of the human race.' So
wrote Barbara Woodhouse in *Talking to Animals* and, as one who
has lived close to animals ever since she was an infant and who
has broken in wild horses, tamed horses in Argentina and at
one point turned horse-dealer, she has had plenty of practical
experience.

Horses have their own individuality. There are no two alike,
and they will prove intractable with a nervous rider, a bully or a
dandy, while yielding with docility and instant understanding to
a confident and considerate rider. On what other animal could
Professor A. F. Tschiffely have made his ride of 1933, famous

in equestrian history? Using only two horses, he rode 10,000 miles from Buenos Aires, the capital of Argentina, to Washington, USA. His journey took him across mountain ranges, deserts, swamps, prairies and forests, in the course of which he met every kind of hazard through every sort of climate; bitter cold, tropical heat, deadly insects, blood-sucking bats and crocodile-infested streams provoked no resistance from either of the two horses he used for his incredible journey. He used one for his baggage and one to ride, changing mounts occasionally. Everybody told Tschiffely that he was mad to attempt the journey and that his horses (Manta and Gato) were hardly tamed and would surely let him down in some way. In fact, he found them perfect companions – hardy, patient, indifferent to the changes in temperature, immune to the illnesses that beset him in the course of his journey.

The three travellers became such friends that, if Tschiffely lay down in his sleeping-bag or slept for the night in some lonely hut, he could with confidence turn the horses loose to roam as they pleased. He knew for a certainty that when he awakened they would be with him. They always were.

They moved at great heights, seemingly unaffected by the rarified air, even at 11,000 feet above sea level. In Peru his horses crossed the River Santa when it was in full flood, a terrifying mass of thundering waters and spume which concealed the treacherous, jagged rocks of the river bed. The local people swore that neither the mad Tschiffely nor his brave horses could make it, but he was so sure of them that he ignored these warnings, and they made their way through the torrents unharmed.

Of the deep bond that exists between master and horse, Tschiffely wrote feelingly and from experience. Would those horses have submitted so endlessly to hazards, discomforts and dangers except for some special rapport or ability to read Tschiffely's thoughts?

An authority on horses, Lady Wentworth, in *Horses in the Making*, writes enthusiastically of their intelligence, reasoning powers and highly developed perception, which today we would call ESP:

To those who live among animals, and especially those who have taught horses and dogs to do tricks, the question as to whether horses or dogs think and reason comes as a surprise, as it seems obvious that they not only think but have various degrees of reasoning power. That they connect cause and effect and act accordingly is indisputable, and also they have a sense of time. This is strong in horses, as every stud groom knows who brings in mares from pasture at feeding time, finding them collected round a gate. Horses also know their respective looseboxes and go into them of their own accord. They can be taught their own names, like dogs, if people will take the trouble to teach them.

They also have a strange sense of someone coming at a distance well out of sight and hearing: once I was riding in the desert with the horizon as a limit all round. My horse suddenly pricked his ears and began fidgeting and neighing. Quite a long time afterwards a horseman galloped up to me. He had been cantering steadily and must have been an incredible distance away when my horse first became aware of him.

Lady Wentworth comes to the conclusion that, considering how many people can neither think nor reason, horses can often beat human beings in common sense.

In many respects, of course, the horse has advantages over a human being in its normal perceptions. Although it probably does not perceive the same range of colours, it can distinguish a few colours. But the horse's vision is superior to that of a human, since it can see in front, to the sides and to the rear. It can even see straight forward and straight backward at the same time. Also the ears of a horse can move independently of each other. But, even allowing for these heightened sensibilities, experts who have spent their lives handling horses have maintained that they possess extra-sensory perception.

When Professor Gustav Wolf, a Basel psychiatrist, declared in 1914 that animals possessed some mysterious source of knowledge and awareness, he was laughed at by all but a few. He was talking of, amongst other cases, the extraordinary story of 'Clever Hans', a horse which, at the turn of the century, proved his capacity to answer questions and solve problems put to him by human beings.

All the facts about 'Clever Hans' show that this was not

another circus act. Certainly the horse had been trained to listen in, and respond to, questions put to him by human beings. But this was not a case of mere conditioned reflexes. Most people know nowadays what a 'conditioned reflex' is: an association of ideas created in the mind of man or animal by which a response becomes automatic. It is a technique perfected and applied by most dictatorships in moulding populations to their will – a useful and sinister supplement to the paraphernalia of physical suppression.

The case of what has come down in parapsychological history as that of the Elberfield Horses, which included Clever Hans, has never been proved or even suspected to be due to fraud or deception of any kind. Hence Professor Wolf's comment: 'Once again something truly great, something overwhelming, has been accomplished outside the limits of organized science. And, as with everything new, it has to fight against the dogmas of the school and the Church.'

The story started in Elberfield, Germany. A horse-fancier named Wilhelm von Osten, using only kindness and patience, trained his horses to think out problems and give their answers by tapping with their hooves on a wooden stool or on the floor. The stallion, Hans, who became known as Clever Hans, learned numbers, and the numbers of letters of the alphabet as represented by their order of sequence.

Von Osten was naturally pleased with the horse's progress but rather startled to discover that Hans had begun to demonstrate capacities which he had not been taught at all. For example, when Osten wrote 35 plus 15 on the blackboard, Hans tapped out 50 without the slightest hesitation. News of this reached the Kaiser, who appointed a commission to enquire into the horse's exploits. Doctors, animal-trainers, zoologists and others observed at close range over a long period and came up with the answer: 'It can't be calculation. Somehow, but we don't know how, the horse is getting signals from its trainers.'

Now, as regards signals, there is a way in which horses, and other animals too, can be made to give correct answers to mathematical queries by means of their paws or hoofs. Briefly, it consists of teaching the animal to paw the ground, because it is hungry, when it smells food. It can be trained to stop pawing or tapping by some almost indistinguishable signal – a slight movement of the hand, the whip raised at a particular angle, even some gesture such as the trainer turning his head to left or right. So a question is put, and when the horse has tapped the correct number of times, the secret signal is given for the horse to stop.

Within two years of training, Clever Hans had progressed to the point when he could indicate the day and date of the month, solve mathematical equations and read an elementary musical script. Von Osten was excited and thrilled with these achievements, but the implied threat to the supremacy of man sparked off such a fusillade of academic abuse and hostility that he became deeply depressed with it all.

Despite his dejection, however, von Osten was determined that his impending death should not bring an end to his experiments, and before he died in 1904 he took on a partner, Karl Krall, a friend and wealthy jeweller. He taught Krall all he knew about training horses and entrusted to him all the carefully kept records of training and results. Krall, who now owned Clever Hans, decided to educate two other horses called Muhamed and Zarif. Thus, Hans, Muhamed and Zarif became known as the Elberfield Horses.

The two newcomers to this strange school (for von Osten had maintained that Clever Hans's education approximated that of a fourteen-year-old schoolboy!) soon proved themselves to be prodigies. They learned things at a fantastic rate and were able to do division and subtraction within a mere two weeks.

Soon psychologists, scientists and others were flocking to Elberfield. They were curious to see what was going on, though apprehensive that admissions as to what they saw might earn them the damaging reputation of being credulous.

Krall introduced improvements in the physical means by which the horses in his care could communicate their thoughts. He designed a chart comprising forty-nine squares, showing the letters, vowels and diphthongs in the German Language. A horse would indicate a letter by striking with his hoof on the appropriate square. The eminent Swiss psychologist Clarparede, who left a very detailed account of the Elberfield horses, describes how Krall put on the blackboard the following mathematical problem: multiply the square root of 49 with the square root of 36. Muhamed, having at first indicated 52, quickly corrected himself and came up with the answer – 42. The psychologist then asked that Muhamed should twice give the square root of 614,656. Muhamed came up with the answer almost at once – 28.

In writing his report, Clarparede explored all possible explanations. He excluded fraud. The closest observations over a long period had failed to reveal any. Of Krall's honesty there was not the least doubt.

One contemporary celebrity who took a deep interest in the Elberfield horses was the Belgian writer Maurice Maeterlinck, Nobel Peace Prize winner in 1911, a great lover of animals, and a founder of the French psychical research society. He records his shocked incredulity when Muhamed, who could speak short but intelligible sentences, greeted him with 'How do you do?' The shock, Maeterlinck recorded at the time, 'came like a breath from the abyss as my mind floundered for a reply. It was as if I had heard a voice from the dead!'

Maeterlinck gives a long and detailed account of his sessions with the Elberfield horses in *The Unknown Guest*. 'The miracle,' he says, 'comes as a surprise, the moment we set foot in it, a sort of instinctive aberration seizes us, refusing to accept the evidence and compelling us to search in every direction to see if there is not another outlet. Even in the presence of these astounding horses, and while they are working before our eyes, we do not yet sincerely believe that which fills and subdues our gaze.'

One scientist declared that the horse's usual mental state was almost akin to that of a man walking in his sleep, and that these bursts of mental activity were 'psychic flashes'. Maeterlinck thought it a 'miracle' that these 'psychic flashes' could be induced and prolonged at will.

Surely one of the strangest accounts in the whole brief history of psychical research is Maeterlinck's description of his 'conversation' with the stallion Muhamed:

One day Krall and his collaborator, Dr Scholler, thought they would try and teach Muhamed to express himself in speech. The horse, a docile and eager pupil, made touching and fruitless efforts to reproduce human sounds. Suddenly he stopped, and his strange phonetic spelling, declared, by striking his foot on the spring-board: '*Ig hb kein gud sdim* – I have not a good voice.'

Observing that he did not open his mouth, they strove to make him understand, by the example of a dog, with pictures, and so on, that in order to speak it is necessary to separate the jaws. They next asked him: 'What must you do to speak?' He replied, by striking with his foot, 'Open mouth'. 'Why, then, don't you open yours?' his questioners next asked. His reply (again by taps) was '*Weil kan nigid* – because I can't'.

Small wonder that Maeterlinck concluded: 'There is probably in the horse, and probably in all that lives on earth, a psychic power similar to that which is hidden beneath the well of our reason.'

'Lady', a telepathic horse also able to do sums, attracted widespread attention from 1927 onwards, at a time when Dr and Mrs Rhine had come, with Professor McDougall, to work at Duke University. Lady was a year-old filly, owned by Mrs Claudia Fonda of Richmond, Virginia, who first intimated that the horse was 'psychic' came one day when she was thinking about it, and it came cantering up to her. It might well have been coincidence, so Mrs Fonda tried thinking of Lady on other occasions – with exactly the same result. This happened too often to be explained away by chance.

Dr Rhine was then in his initial stages of research into ESP in human beings but had never believed that ESP need be the monopoly of humans. The chance of investigating an alleged case of psychic capacities in a horse was, therefore, of great interest to him. The investigators were able to persuade the owner to withdraw from the scene of the tests, so that any possibility of voluntary or involuntary signalling could be scientifically ruled out. Lady had been trained to answer questions by pointing with her nose to letters and numbers on a special apparatus. These tests, during which the horse gave correct answers to questions without any possibility of the investigators 'giving the game away' by gestures, demonstrate that she had some sort of extra-sensory perception. Did she pick up the answers by telepathy?

But Lady's most spectacular success came in a murder hunt. A friend of the district attorney of Norfolk County, Massachusetts, asked the horse about a boy who had been missing from his home for several months. The horse gave as the answer 'Pittsfield Water Wheel'. This conveyed little, except to a police captain, who decided that the horse was trying to say 'Field and Wilde Water Pitt' – an abandoned quarry. A search was made, and the boy's body was found there. On one occasion Lady spelled a word she had never heard, 'engine'. A minute later a tractor rattled its way down the road. This was considered a form of precognition. Then Lady gave another, even more spectacular, example by predicting correctly the outcome of the 1927 Dempsey-Sharkey fight!

Small wonder that Dr Robert L. Morris, Co-ordinator of Research at the Psychical Research Foundation, Durham, North Carolina, declared recently: 'Evidence that ESP is present in other species than our own is considerable.'

A Welsh researcher, Henry Blake, of the Llanybyther Horse Centre, has studied horses and their ESP communication for over twenty years, and out of 120 experiments in thought-transference which he conducted with the assistance of his wife, he got positive results in eighty-one cases.

Henry Blake is convinced, from his long observation and handling of horses and from the detailed, lengthy and careful experiments he has carried out, that horses possess ESP by which they can communicate, and receive, thought images, transmitting them to other animals and to human beings. He believes that horses can operate 'mental radio' over considerable distances and, using techniques based on this proposition, he has rejected the more rough-and-ready, dramatic methods of 'breaking-in' for the less spectacular but equally effective method (to use his own phrase) of 'gentling' horses. This business of establishing rapport and trust between horse and owner enables him to make a horse docile and a friend within an hour.

In *Talking with Horses*, he relates from his own experience how

ESP can convey emotions such as anger, affection and a sense of danger. Once a friend brought him an Arab-cross-Welsh six-year-old stallion for gentling. Blake felt an immediate affinity with his charge, and complete confidence between them was soon established. Nevertheless, when a friend came to stay with him, and he was allowed to ride the stallion, Henry Blake *knew*, from a sort of knotting feeling in his stomach, that something was going wrong. Taking his car, he followed and caught up with the horse and rider, by now four miles away, to find that the horse was going 'all over the place, just ready to explode'. He was in time to whip his friend off the saddle and put his daughter on in his place, and the two went off quite happily.

Henry Blake has described how he evolved his own technique of 'gentling'. It is a good coined word, for it consists of taking a quiet but confident approach to a nervous or fierce horse. Sometimes he will merely stand still, with a bucket of food, and let the horse come to him. Or he will approach the frightened or hostile horse slowly and quietly, speaking to him in a sing-song voice. He gets near enough to caress the horse with the tips of his fingers, simulating the mother's muzzle reassuring a foal, or use the palm of his hand to suggest the pressure of another horse's head.

Once trust was created, Henry Blake found he could guide horses merely by *thinking* instructions. One horse whom he called Weeping Roger could pick up his mental pictures by telepathy: 'I would steer him to the left or right simply by visualizing the road. This was the first time I had consciously experienced telepathy with a horse.'

In 'gentling' horses, Henry Blake is continuing, in his own individual way, a long-established country tradition known as 'horse-whispering'. Until some time after the First World War, the horse-whisperer was one of the most respected and sought-after specialists in the farming community. Many a story is told of how, by a single whispered word, the horse-whisperer could transform a fierce and intractible horse into a docile friend. Whisperers were credited with being able to 'will' a horse towards them without moving, and to be able to stop runaways in their tracks.

In Scotland the horse-whisperers jealously guarded their mysterious techniques and were known as 'the Society of the Horseman's Word'.

In the eastern counties of Essex, Suffolk, Norfolk and Lincolnshire, the techniques seem to have involved a degree of superstition or even magic. The whisperer would often carry the bone of a frog or a toad, and a substance steeped in 'drawing oils' which by their pleasant odour strongly attracted the horses (whereas the frog bone repelled them and kept them at bay). But it was 'the word' – the whispered word whose intonation and spelling they alone knew – which was the most common device they used.

The medical aspects of the whisperers' attraction and repellent techniques have never been explored scientifically, although it is common knowledge that there are smells that draw different species and others that they find intolerable. The fascination which the plant catnip has for cats is a case in point. Most of the accounts of horse-whisperers at work do indicate, as proved by Henry Blake many generations later, that thought transmission is possible between horses and human beings.

9

Phantom Horses

Phantom horses haunt the folklore of most countries. Spectral horses, and horses seeing ghosts, are legendary in Britain and elsewhere. Chosen at random from Europe alone, here are a few examples of horses and their masters surviving their natural death.

In the great forest of Fontainebleau, an early French king, Hugh Capet, still rides to hounds in the royal chase. He was said to appear at the palace when one of his successors died a violent death. In England, the royal forest of Windsor is haunted by the ghost of Herne the Hunter, whom we shall meet again. In Sweden, country folk say that Odin (to us, the Saxon god Woden) is passing by when they hear a ghostly cavalcade of carriages and horses' hooves. In Norway, a spectral hunt with riders, horses and hounds in full cry is known as 'the chase of the inhabitants of Asgarth'.

The mountainous regions of Scotland and Wales are haunted by 'Pookas' – on the night of the new moon, these enormous grey horses rise out of the lakes and tarns and go galloping round their shores.

Oxwick church, on the coast of Pembrokeshire, is said to be haunted by the spectre of a 'huge white horse walking on its hind legs', as it was described by a comparatively recent witness. Local legend says that hundreds of years ago a system of horse sacrifice was practised. The head, neck and fore-quarters of the slaughtered animal, with its front legs, were mounted on a pole, taken to the coast and displayed there to scare off invaders.

In *Shropshire Folk-Lore* there is a story of a ghostly colt which shows a proper respect for religion. About the middle of the last century a lady was buried in her jewels at Fitz, then robbed by the parish clerk. Thereafter, according to local beliefs, she used to walk in a spot known as Cuthery Hollow in the form of a colt, known locally as Obrick's Colt. One night the thieving clerk met the shadowy figure and in his terror knelt upon his knees pleading: 'Abide, Satan, abide! I am a righteous man and a psalm singer!'

In such tales there are faint echoes of ancient religious beliefs and rites. In other ghost stories, the Devil plays his part, either directly or through his human agents, the witches.

On Bodmin Moor in Cornwall, a wicked seventeenth-century magistrate, Jan Tregeagle, who sold his soul to the devil, was ordered to spend all eternity emptying Dozmary Pool with a perforated shell. Every now and then, the Devil arrives with a pack of headless hounds to set him back still further by chasing him across the moor.

In the Scottish capital, Edinburgh, the ghost of a warlock, Major Weir, who was burned in 1670, is to be seen riding through West Bow, on a flaming, headless horse. He is accompanied by his sister, a witch with a sinister reputation.

Some say Herne the Hunter himself was a warlock who hanged himself to avoid the bonfire reserved in his day for servants of the Devil. When Shakespeare introduced Herne and the oak where he died into *The Merry Wives of Windsor*, his ghost had already been around for centuries. He is thought to have been a royal forester under Richard II, who won his position by saving the King's life. He had thrown himself in front of the King who was being charged by a wounded stag at bay. This version of the legend – an ugly tale of royal ingratitude – relates that Herne himself was wounded by the stag and never fully recovered from his injuries. Eventually he grew emfeebled and was dismissed from the royal service. Heartbroken, he hanged himself in the forest he had ruled.

The village of Markyate in Hertfordshire, about five miles from Luton, has a ghostly horse and rider with an interesting history. To the north of the church lies Markyate Cell, a mansion which incorporates the original monk's cell, or hermitage, which once stood there. In 1645 Lady Katharine Ferrers, a beautiful but bloodthirsty aristocrat, used to dress up in highwayman's clothes and hold up travellers at gunpoint. Eventually she was shot during a hold-up and, limping back to her secret hide-out in the mansion, she was discovered dying, and the secret was out. Since then she has occasionally been reported riding her phantom horse.

The belief that horses could see departed spirits was once widely held in Wales, and there are innumerable stories of travellers by horse or stage-coach being frightened at the behaviour of their horses when confronted by the Gwyllgi, 'the dog of darkness' – a fearful spectre of a mastiff with blazing red eyes. It was said to emit so unearthly a howl that travellers fainted outright. The story is told of horses being terrified on a stretch of lane between Mowsiad and Lisworney Crossways, where the Gwyllgi was often seen. A farmer was returning home from market on a young mare when suddenly the animal shied, reared, threw the farmer and bolted for home. The farm workers found the mare trembling by the stable door and, going back for the farmer, found him lying in the mud.

Stories of a 'wild hunt' – a spectral gathering of hunters and dogs – are told in many counties of England and Wales, as well as in Scotland. Sir Arthur Quiller-Couch, in *Folkore of a Cornish Village*, tells of a poor herdsman who was crossing the moors one windy night when he heard coming from the tors the baying of hounds and recognized it as the ghostly dog pack known in the area. But he was still three or four miles from his house. The light was poor, the path indeterminate and difficult to follow, the soil lumpy and damp. The howling of the hounds came nearer until, to his horror, he could see in front of him a ghostly concourse of hunters, their horses and the dogs. They were about to rush upon him when he fell down upon his knees and prayed. He heard the hunter shout '*Bo shrove*' (meaning 'The boy prays') and the ghostly hunt sped away.

W. T. Stead, in *Real Ghost Stories*, gives many accounts of spectral horses. He tells how General Barter, of Careystown, Whitegate, Co. Cork, Ireland, who served in India, saw a spectral cavalcade when he was staying in the hills. He was returning home one evening when he saw a rider and attendants coming towards him. The moon was so bright that one could have read a newspaper by its light, so that General Barter saw the advance of the party as plainly as if it had been noon. The party drew nearer:

> On the party came, until almost in front of me. The rider was in full dinner dress, with white waistcoat, and wearing a tall, chimney-pot hat, and he sat on a powerful hill pony (dark brown, with mane and tail), in a listless sort of way, the reins hanging loosely from both hands. . . .
>
> A Syce led the pony on each side, but their faces I could not see, the one next to me having his back to me, and the one farthest off being hidden by the pony's head. . . . I called out in Hindustani *'Quon hai?'* (who is it?) There was no answer, and as they came right in front of me I said, in English 'Hullo, what the devil do you want here?'

General Barter had recognized the rider as a lieutenant he knew – but the face looked like that of a dead man and, instead of being clean-shaven as usual, it was surrounded by a fringe, once known as the Newgate fringe. The General dashed up the bank, gained the road, stood on the spot where the group had been – and it had disappeared, men, pony and all. They could not have gone on, as the road stopped at a precipice twenty yards further on.

An old Durham miner, Mr T. Gibbon, told me a few years ago of how he had encountered the ghost of a pit pony in a disused mine working. It was in 1919, when it was his job to descend the pit every night to relieve a man at the electric pumps. This incident took place in a worked-out coal seam in which no one was employed but the pumpman.

> On New Year's Eve I went to work as usual at about 9.30 p.m. Before descending the pit I looked in at the turbine house and bid my pal 'Goodnight'. He said: 'I will ring you on the telephone and let you hear the colliery buzzer hooting the old year out between 11.58 and 12.02 a.m.' I got my gunnie (lamp) and went down. From the bottom of the shafts to the pumps was a distance of about 500 yards. When I got to the pump house I sat down for a breather, but I had only sat down for a few seconds when I saw a large moth flying around. I had a good look at it and discovered it to be a Death's-Head

Moth. I tried to knock it down with my cloth cap, and after chasing it for about five yards I got tired of it and sat down to get my wind. I was at the cross-road, and directly in front of me the road turned to the right and inclined. On my right a manhole (recess) was cut from the coal face. As I sat in solitude and deathly silence I heard the distinct patter of a pony's hooves and harness and chains approaching. The row stopped, and an arm lunged out of the manhole and grabbed at the pony, which turned around and went back into the mine.

Exchanging a New Year drink with his friend later, Mr Gibbon told of his experience and begged his friend to keep it secret. Three months later he asked the enginewright whether, on any occasion, anyone had been hurt or killed in the disused mine seam. The enginewright, giving him a keen look, told him that, 'A laddie was killed there on New Year's Eve, while trying to stop a runaway pony.' Even later, while mending a wireless set for a friend, he was relating his experience, when the friend said, 'Aye lad, that's reet, ah was there at the time and helped to carry him out.'

A story of a phantom horse and rider is told by Elliott O'Donnell in *Animal Ghosts*. A doctor was summoned by a friend to a bad accident, in which both horse and rider had been injured. Mounting his horse, the doctor rode swiftly to the scene but, on his way, heard a shot fired and then saw his friend riding towards him at a furious pace, on a wretched-looking chestnut horse. On his arrival at the house, the butler told him that the man had died and that the horse, being badly injured, had been shot.

In 1927 the *Daily News* printed an extraordinary story suggesting that horses, besides being telepathic, have some sort of psychokinesis (physical force conveyed by mental energy). The writer described how, one January night, just after midnight, he and several members of his family were startled by several extremely heavy knocks on the front door. He immediately jumped out of bed, slipped on his dressing-gown and left the bedroom; on his way downstairs he found that his father had also been awakened by the same noise and was, like him, going to investigate.

It was a beautiful moonlight night, and the snow lay thick on the ground. From the landing window, there was nobody in sight, and the snow seemed undisturbed. When they reached ground-floor level and unlocked, they found absolute peace and quiet outside and not a trace of any footprints anywhere around the house. Nor had there been anybody there, for there was nothing to suggest that the brass knocker had been interfered with in any way, and there was no sign of the gate leading into the road having been opened – had there been, there would have been lines in the snow caused by the opening of it, for the snow was thick and above the bottom level of the gate.

Father and son retired to bed, bewildered by the thunderous knocks. They were not disturbed again that night, but the following morning the son, on visiting the stable to attend to his horse as usual, found him lying dead.

In my book *Ghosts and Hauntings*, I have given many instances of deaths being signalled by loud knocks of this description, or of the simultaneous appearance of a ghost to some close friend or relative of the person who has just died. Heatherleigh Hall, near Carlisle, waas said for generations to be visited occasionally by a ghostly rider, the thundering of his horse's hooves being distinctly heard as he raced by. He was what is known for convenience as a 'death visitant' – one whose coming invariably presages a death in the family. There were several instances of a death following his reported appearances.

'Wicked' Will Darrell, whose cruel murder of a newborn child is said to be responsible for the haunting of Littlecote Manor in Wiltshire, has many times been reported riding his spectral horse when night has fallen.

The story is that on a stormy night in 1575 he sent his servants to fetch a midwife, Mrs Barnes, from her home in Great Shefford, and she was brought, blindfolded, to his manor, where she was unmasked after she had been taken through the entrance and up a flight of stairs, the number of which she counted on her way. She was then taken into a chamber where a masked woman lay in the last extremities of labour. The most elementary requirements of a delivery were lacking – no clean linen or other needs. Despite the inhuman and primitive conditions in which she had to do her work, under threat of death if she did not, the baby was delivered. Wicked Will Darrell then seized the baby and, ignoring the frantic pleas of the midwife, threw it into the glowing embers of a huge fire and crushed it in with his boot.

Mrs Barnes was threatened with death if she ever disclosed what she knew and was then blindfolded again and conducted back to her home. Her conscience, however, would not let her rest, and she later revealed what had happened. Will Darrell's house was identified by the number of stairs she had counted when blindfolded, and a piece of curtaining which she had surreptitiously torn off as evidence of her visit. However, although Will Darrell was brought to trial, he went unpunished because, probably, he bribed the judge. One day, while riding near a spot known today as Darrell's Stile, his horse shied as they saw the ghost of the murdered baby, and Darrell was killed. It is said he still rides, and ghosts have often been seen in and around the house for years.

The ghost of a horse bearing his headless master has occasionally been seen in recent years at High Down, Pirton, which lies about three miles north-west of Hitchin, in Hertfordshire, and has sometimes been seen at the priory, which is also haunted by a ghost known as the Grey Lady. During the Civil War there was an encounter between Roundheads and Cavaliers on the borders of Hertfordshire and Bedfordshire, in which Cromwell's soldiers won the day. The defeated Cavalier leader, Goring, took flight and found refuge with his friends, the Docwras family of High Down. He was tracked by Cromwell's men and, although for a time he evaded them by hiding in the hollow trunk of an elm tree, he was discovered and executed on the spot with a sword. He is said to ride on every 15 June from High Down to Hitchin with his head in his hands.

Perhaps because the execution of Charles I and the Civil War were historically such traumatic events, a considerable number of hauntings involving horses and their riders are connected with the Roundheads and Cavaliers. Cromwell himself is said to have been seen riding down a lane close to Naseby Field.

One of the strangest ghost stories involving horses is a link with the Peninsular War (1808-14) when the Duke of Wellington, then Sir Arthur Wellesley, dug himself in behind the lines of Torres Vedras and sent home to Britain for a pack of hounds, so that his officers might have some exercise in hunting. It was strange, in the midst of a war, to see the soldiers in their red, green and blue uniforms, accompanied by servants in brilliant red, galloping away after hounds. But not so strange as the fact that many local inhabitants have since seen and heard a ghost pack, in full cry before a band of huntsmen in vivid uniforms, similar in every detail to those worn during the Peninsular War.

10

The Mysterious Dolphin

Normally Bob Holman, a plumber turned deep sea diver and currently looking after a National Trust property near Bodmin in Cornwall, is at his home, Smugglers Cove, Portreath, Cornwall, where for a long time he ran a diving school. He still teaches and dives, but there is now a sad element in his life and thought which he cannot shake off. Percy, the fourteen-foot-long dolphin who befriended him and was for long his constant and much-loved companion, has gone out to sea and not come back.

When Bob Holman returns home, he looks fondly out to sea, hoping against hope to catch a glimpse again of that triangular fin, longing to swim out to the dolphin and sport about in the water, as they used to, longing to stroke that great, strong snout of his, strong enough to kill a shark with a single blow, yet never to be feared where men, women or children were concerned. How often did Robert, his son, play with Percy! So, too, did his daughter, Deborah.

'I really do miss him,' he told me, sadly. 'When I go home, I look out to sea, wondering if he will ever appear again. It's like missing a relative . . .'

But before Percy, there was Beaky. Dear Beaky! How the children of Cornwall loved him! He was sheer Disney – the stuff of wholesome fairy-tales come true, playing with them, giving them free rides on his huge back, showing always the zest and sense of mischief that have made the dolphin a legend in history, imprinted its form on coins of the ancient world, caused monuments to be raised in memory of its friendship with man.

'Years ago' (it was actually in the early seventies) 'I was teaching diving at a club in Portreath and we used to go wherever

Beaky was. He saved four or five people from drowning – more than people know. There was a foreign sailor who fell off the side of a boat and he held him up for several hours until help arrived. On another occasion one of my diving pals was diving off Lands End when a fog came down and he became separated from his boat, and Beaky actually took him to the steps of his diving boat, where he wanted to go. It was an incredible experience really. That was at Falmouth.'

Beaky came to the coast of Cornwall in the early seventies, after enjoying himself, and giving his friends enormous pleasure, off the Isle of Man. There he was nicknamed Donald by a diver called Moira, but when the harbour there became a noisy place because of explosions caused in the course of reconstruction, Donald swam off to Cornwall in disgust to escape the noisy chaos. There he became known as Beaky.

Dr Horace Dobbs got to know Beaky (Donald) during a diving holiday in the Isle of Man in September 1974. Although he had been shot in the head by one of the fishermen, he frolicked and played in local waters, showing the friendliness and curiosity characteristic of the breed. Despite his bulk and strength, he was as gentle as a kitten with his human friends.

The following year Horace Dobbs returned to the Isle of Man, taking with him a ciné-camera to film the dolphin he had come to love. Donald lost no time, once Dobbs was in the water, in coming up to him, pushing his snout against the camera mounting and showing curiosity as to what it could be. Meanwhile, Dr Dobbs' son, Ashley, was snorkling down to take photographs. This sent the dolphin into frenzies of excitement and he was soon leaping in and out of the water within inches of the boy. It seemed to Dr Dobbs that he was moving towards his son with such force that he might not control himself as well as usual. He surfaced, intending to tell his son to get away from the dolphin and into the dinghy, but as he surfaced, to quote Dr Dobbs' own words: 'Ashley rose gently out of the water, sitting astride the dolphin's head.' Ashley had a broad grin on his face and held both hands in the air as Donald carried him at speed across the harbour. Later Ashley explained that this exciting experience happened not by his planning or initiative but by the dolphin, which had reared up underneath him, adroitly supported him and sped away.

Beaky disappeared from the Cornish scene in 1978. The last time Bob Holman saw him, he was suffering from two shotgun wounds and, during a terrific storm, it is assumed he was swept out to sea. It is ironic and sad that a friendly animal that trusted human beings and had saved the lives of four of them should have been murdered by one of their kind. A careful tab is kept on the bodies of dolphins washed ashore, as they are a protected species, and their measurements are taken in an attempt to identify any that have become known. Despite legal protection, dolphins are sometimes destroyed for sheer 'fun' by fishermen. One was blown up in New Zealand and another in Corunna in recent times.

It is particularly sad that some fishermen seem impelled to attack dolphins, because not only does it not happen in reverse (no dolphin has ever been known to attack a human being) but dolphins actually *help* fishermen with their catches. Pliny the Elder (AD 23-79) marvelled at the dolphin's speed and intelligence, noting its friendliness to man. So did Aristotle the Greek philosopher (384-322 BC).

Oppian, a Green poet of the third century AD, describes the skill with which the dolphins hunt for fish and the help they actually give human fishermen whom they recognize as relations having the same purpose. Pliny the Elder mentioned a region of Nimes in the province of Narbonne where there was a marsh called Latera 'where dolphins catch fish in partnership with a human fisherman'. At a regular season shoals of mullet rush from the narrow mouth of the marsh in to the sea, which would make it impossible for nets to be spread across the channel and in any case their immense weight would break the nets. The dolphins, he recorded, would 'round up' the mullet, driving the scared fishes into the shallow waters, where they were more easily caught.

Oppian describes how Greek fishermen were helped by dolphins off the shores of the island of Euboea, near Athens. The fishermen would light flares at night, which would attract the fish. The dolphins would come up too. The fish in their terror would attempt to swim out to sea, but an outer ring of dolphins drove them back, bringing them close to land, where they were easily caught by a trident. Then, 'The dolphins draw near and ask the guerdon of their friendship, even their allotted portion of the spoil . . . and the fishers deny them not but gladly give them a share of their successful fishing . . .'

Dolphins still help fishermen in Brazil in the same way as they have done for centuries. A Swedish naturalist, Dr Lars Ofgren, described in a lecture at Brockington College, Hull, in 1985 how he had witnessed shoals of dolphin driving the fish into Brazilian nets.

The link between dolphins and mankind is one of evolution. The dolphin is not a fish but a mammal – that is, it conceives its young one at a time and suckles them by nipple. It is descended from extinct land mammals which, far back in time, took to the water. Naturalists call this group of sea animals cetaceans, whose ancestral relationship to ourselves may be seen in the fact that vestigial thigh bones and tibia still remain as part of their construction.

Bottle-nosed dolphins, the variety most often encountered in aquaria, seem to have a kind of fixed smile, due to the curled edges of the mouth and the blunt snout. Their eyes are bright and intelligent and, as all divers attest, change their expression at close quarters, sometimes giving an impression of curiosity or of humour – but always of friendliness. A dolphin never attacks a human being, despite its great bulk and power. Come to that, it never attacks its young. Dolphins love and protect their young to such a degree that all the females gather round to watch the birth of a baby dolphin and stay around to protect it from marauders, especially sharks.

There is another well-known species (*Delphinus delphis*) which has a sharper beak than the bottle-nosed dolphin, moves in deeper waters and takes less kindly to captivity. It is this species which is usually seen playing around the bows of ocean-going ships. For thousands of years their playfulness and friendliness to human beings have made them seem like a lucky omen. They never attacked men and, playing and frisking by the boat, they seemed at times to be leading it safely on its way.

The old Greek legend which maintained that dolphins once were men and that this accounted for the rapport between the two, wherever and in whatever circumstances they met, has, like most legends, some basis in fact. Dr John C. Lilly, a neurophysiologist who became interested in dolphins two decades ago, did much research at Marineland, in Florida, and helped to construct a dolphin research station at Nazareth Bay, St Thomas, in the Virgin Islands, says flatly that dolphins are *more* intelligent than human beings and have a strong psychic sense. Dolphins, he points out, have existed for millions of years – long before man. The dolphin brain has been developing far longer than man's. 'A first-class brain' is how Dr Lilly describes it.

As early as 1948 D. O. Hebb, an American authority on dolphins, placed the dolphin's intelligence well up in the animal scale, and ever since neurologists, scientists and others have argued with increasing bitterness as to whether the dolphin's intelligence is equal to, or in some respects superior to, human intelligence. It needs saying that those who commit themselves to claims that the dolphin's intelligence is in many respects superior to ours come almost exclusively from those who had had long and intimate contact with dolphins – people who follow scientific methods of observation, such as Dr Lilly. Much of the hositility to the 'pro-dolphin' school is similar to that manifested when Darwin first promulgated his ideas on the evolution of man and dared to say that we could be descended from the apes. Such hostility is based not so much upon science as on vain indignation that any species, in any respect, could be thought superior to man.

The brains of dolphins, if one compares the mass of brain with the mass of body, are broadly similar to those of men, and the folding of the cerebral hemispheres is also similar. Their hearing is remarkably acute, far better than that of human beings. The dolphin, in its own language, emits a 'click click', which appears to be a sort of echo-sounding or sonar system, identifying the nature and situation of objects, fish or men. Dolphins have, in fact, many sounds, by which they can communicate with each other, with fish and, according to Dr Lilly, with human beings too. He has maintained that dolphins attempt to imitate human laughter (and since they like to play with human beings, especially children, they hear plenty of that). He has heard a series of sounds like 'hah-hah-hah's' a few seconds after a woman has laughed. He observed dolphins trying to imitate human whistling, or the whistle-type noises emitted by electronic equipment. He has even stated that dolphins attempt to imitate human speech: 'I have heard most distinctly the following words and phrases "copied" in an extremely high-pitched and brief fashion: "Three-two-three", "Tee ar Pee" (the letters TRP had just been given) and a host of others, less clear but verging so closely on humanlike rhythm, enunciation and phonetic quality as to be eerie.'

A strange story suggesting that a rapport of some mysterious kind exists between dolphins and humans is told by Dr Lilly in connection with a dolphin called Lizzie, at the Marineland Aquarium. On 16 April 1960 Lizzie was very ill. Dr Lilly and his colleagues were trying to take care of her, and pondering what to do, when over the loudspeaker system came the call to dinner: 'It's six o'clock!' There was a peremptory note to the announcement, because there was a chance of missing the meal if they didn't come right away. Dr Lilly never saw Lizzie alive again, for she died soon afterwards, but on listening to tape recordings of the sounds in the Institute, he was astonished to hear, after the announcement 'It's six o'clock', a realistic imitation of it in dolphin 'language'. But closer listening, again and again, to the sounds, made them sound more like 'It's a trick!'

The unusual intelligence of dolphins was proved when he was experimenting to discover the nature of the different areas of the dolphin's brain for, as with humans, these have different functions. Thus, there is a 'pleasure area': as with experiments with human beings, electrodes capable of stimulating the brain at different points, were planted, and the 'pleasure-area' having been stimulated, the dolphin, responding with whistles, grating noises, barks and wet kisses, had carefully noted what Dr Lilly had done. As he quickly devised a set of levers by which the dolphin could 'spark off' these pleasurable sensations on her own, and was trying to complete his task, the dolphin sailed in at great speed and pushed her snout just where she was supposed to. The dolphin had 'guessed' what Dr Lilly was up to, for such a game had not hitherto been devised. She was quicker on the uptake than a human being would have been. How? Was it guesswork, or do dolphins read thoughts from human brains by some means undiscovered by us?

A Russian researcher, Dr Yablokov, after studying the brains of dolphins and their behaviour, has stated categorically that there is something unique, and mysterious, about the dolphin's brain:

> There is considerable evidence to support the view that dolphins *are radically different* from other members of the animal world. The question arises: 'What is a dolphin? And what is his relationship to man? . . .'
>
> . . . human society is the most highly complex group that we know of. But that of the dolphins, too, is extraordinarily complex. Suffice it to say that up to ten generations coexist at one time in dolphin societies. If that were the case with man, Leonardo da Vinci, Lomonovov, Faraday and Einstein would still be alive. Could not the dolphin's brain contain an amount of information comparable in volume to the thousands of tons of books in our libraries? Whatever our opinion of the dolphin, it will not be more than a human judgement due to the limitations on our knowledge.

It was Dr Yablokov and his colleague in research, Ivan Belkovitch, who discovered, as a result of autopsies on dead dolphins, that these animals can die, like humans, of heart attacks and coronary thrombosis. They can die from worry and tension – one, imprisoned at the Marine Sciences Division of the Naval Missile Centre in California, suffered a stomach haemorrhage brought on by tension, presumably from the unhappiness of being captive.

That dolphins are capable of tender and affectionate feelings and that deprivation of love, or of an object of love, can reduce them to despair and to self-neglect making death inevitable (a kind of suicide), have been proved by those who have studied dolphin behaviour closely. There is the well-known case of a dolphin that died of a broken heart. There is absolutely no doubt about the cause. The claim is not based on speculation. The facts are these:

According to a paper in the *Journal of Mammology*, by David H. Brown and Kenneth S. Norris, a small female dolphin was captured by means of a hook placed in a tank. The hook injured her, and the shock of capture and of being wounded were so great that she could scarcely keep herself afloat. Dolphins, being mammals, must come up for air and cannot live without it. Therefore glass jars were attached to her to act as floats. It was touch and go whether she would live, she seemed so aimless and dispirited. She merely floated about, and her captors were sure she would die soon unless they could think something up quickly.

How about a male companion, they thought? They brought in a male *Delphinus*. Pauline, as they named the female, showed favourable reactions to the newcomer, making the sounds which are recognizable to researchers as indicating acceptance. Despite the shock and pain of her injury, she even made some effort to swim. The bottles were removed. The male dolphin tried to help Pauline to swim, pushing under her and bringing her to the surface. This he did with infinite patience, again and again.

Pauline recovered. The two dolphins became inseparable, swimming happily around together, playing games, showing every sign of affection. Two months later Pauline died from an infection of the wound that was caused during her capture. As she died, her companion circled round her constantly, emitting a shrill whistle of distress. When she was dead he continued his cries, swimming round and round for three days, refusing all food. Then he, too, died. An autopsy showed an ulcerous condition aggravated by his refusal to eat. Peritonitis followed, and proved fatal. His ceaseless lamentations after Pauline's death were one of the saddest displays ever witnessed in dolphin research. Nor is such affection confined to dolphins of the opposite sex. Male friends separated, sometimes for months, have greeted each other with extravagant demonstrations of joy and affection.

Every story about dolphins, every report, from no matter what country or in which period, confirms the rapport which dolphins feel towards human beings. Small wonder that the ancient

Greeks believed that dolphins once were men. Over 20,000 years before the birth of Christ, some artist of palaeolithic times drew dolphins and men together in the cave of Levanzo, in the Engadi Islands off Sicily. As long ago as that, dolphins and men had an affinity. But men at that time were primitive; dolphins had behind them millions of years of development, possessing faculties and thought processes which, even today, impress and mystify us.

Let us ask why, without some mystical attraction, a dolphin *should* feel impelled to rescue from death someone of another species, somebody never seen before. Dolphins have to kill for food. Their huge mouths conceal a formidable array of razor-sharp teeth – yet they never bite a human being, not even if attacked. We may ask why a lawyer's wife swimming off a Florida beach in 1949, drawn out to sea by a series of mighty waves, should have been saved from death by a dolphin. As she took in water and was drowning, she found herself 'pushed violently from behind, and I landed on the beach with my nose in the sand . . . in the water, twenty feet from shore, a dolphin was jumping and swimming in circles'. Eleven years later, off the same stretch of coast, a swimmer who was in difficulties found herself 'guided' by a dolphin which nudged her away from the dangerous currents and deeper waters into the safety of shallower waters.

There are still some people alive today who can remember one of the most famous and best-loved dolphins of all time, Pelorus Jack. He was of a species of dolphin different from those most commonly encountered – not a *Delphinus* or a *Tursiops* but a *Grampus griseus*, lacking the beak which is so familiar and expected a feature of the dolphins painted by artists, carved on monuments and fountains and incised in ancient seals. Pelorus Jack was one of the friendliest dolphins ever. He was also the subject of a Government edict ensuring his personal protection, so popular was he and so apprehensive were his friends that someone might steal him for a zoo or private collection.

For over twenty years, from 1880 onwards, Pelorus Jack accompanied ships crossing Cook Strait, on the run between Wellington and Nelson, New Zealand in an area off Pelorus Sound, from which he derived his name. Near the entrance to the sound, he would join the Nelson-bound vessel and keep it company until it reached French Pass, a channel separating d'Urville Island from the mainland. He would do the same on the reverse journey by another vessel. As soon as he heard the throb of a ship's engines, he would move swiftly to the scene, jumping in the air again and again, to the delight of the passengers, some of whom knew him and would cry, as they espied his huge form leaping towards them: 'Here he comes!'

Pelorus Jack had once been fired on by *The Penguin* and somehow, even from afar, he knew it as the one vessel he would not go near. Strangely, *The Penguin* sank in 1909 with the loss of seventy-five lives, adding substance to the long-held superstition (held particularly by the ancients) that misfortune would surely attend anyone who harmed a dolphin. It is interesting, as an example of the attraction which humans have for dolphins, that although one ship had nearly killed it, it still accompanied the others, gambolling and frolicking before the passengers as though enjoying their interest and their excited cries of admiration. Forgiveness, we like to think, is a human quality; yet Pelorus Jack, who had a good memory, forgave those who injured him.

Issuing a government edict against the molesting or abducting of Pelorus Jack was not a simple matter, for he had first to be identified. Hundreds had seen him; nobody had handled him. But in 1904 cameras were not in general use, and on 6 September the Governor of New Zealand, Lord Plunkett, issued an Order in Council making it unlawful 'during the period of five years from the date of the gazetting of these regulations . . . to take the fish or mammal of the species commonly known as Risso's dolphin (*Grampus griseus*) in the waters of the Cook Strait, or of the bays, sounds or estuaries thereto'.

Nobody knows for certain about the passing of Pelorus Jack. He disappeared in 1912, some say killed by harpooners with a fleet of Norwegian whalers which anchored off the entrance to Pelorus Sound on 20 April 1912. There are others who believe that he died of natural causes.

What is certain is that Pelorus Jack was missed far more than most human beings. Hundreds of children, and adults too, who had regarded him as friend and companion of the seas for so many years, could hardly accept that he was no more. Sir Sidney Harmer, a famous authority on whales in the twenties, who was then President of the Linnean Society in London, told the society, which had completed a report on Pelorus Jack in 1929: 'In the light of this story we may have to review our incredulity in regard to the classical narratives of the friendliness of dolphins towards mankind.'

11

Ape and Essence
(Title of a book by Aldous Huxley)

In a homely apartment high up in a Manhattan skyscraper lives a young, intelligent woman whose best friend is a small capuchin monkey whose name is Henrietta but whom her owner calls Henry.

Without this attractive, lively and highly intelligent animal Sue Strong's life would be a misery. She is a paraplegic. And in an amazing way, the little monkey protects, assists and comforts her mistress, performing countless tasks that require a quick intelligence.

Sue Strong is not alone in the world. She has sisters and parents. Yet, she cheerfully admits, the little monkey is as much a member of her family as the rest of them.

The capuchin monkey is part of a training project initiated by Dr Mary Joan Willard of New York's Albert Einstein College of Medicine, and the project has been to train monkeys to assist paraplegics in much the same way as guide dogs are trained to help the blind. The analogy is a good one, since master and animal are held close by a bond of real affection and understanding, a cheerful and total dedication of duty to another, to an individual.

Sue lives in a wheelchair. When she sleeps, she has to be plugged into a respirator for her lungs to work. Attached to her wheelchair is an ultra-modern laser device activated by a bar fixed just below her chin, so that she can operate it with a nod. She can flash the laser's red dot on almost anything. If she flashes it on a book, the monkey leaps over to it, fetches it and, placing it on a specially arranged reading-desk, even opens it at the first page. Henrietta then brings her 'mouth stick' – which Sue puts between her teeth to turn pages or to type.

Sue became paralysed thirteen years ago, at the age of twenty-two, when, sleeping in the back of a van, it overturned, damaging her spine irrevocably and making her limbs unusable. When she is taken out in her wheelchair, New Yorkers stare in wonder at her loving and lively companion.

The great controversy which divided the nation when Charles Darwin first suggested we might be descended from apes has largely died out. We are all now free to consider the remarkable similarity between the primates and ourselves without offending those who accept Genesis as received biblical truth. We need no longer ask, as Disraeli once did: 'Ape or angel?'

Long before modern science had got to grips with simian anatomy and physiology, it had struck thinking men that the ape had one thing in common with man – unlike any other animal, he could walk upright on his two hind legs as readily as on all four. The great ape, swinging from branch to branch using his arms, or forelegs, gave way to the baboon described by Buffon in the eighteenth century.

For much of his evidence, Buffon had to rely on travellers' tales, but he gives an eye-witness account of 'the orang-outang which I saw, [which] walked always upright, even when it carried heavy burthens'. He goes on to describe instances of this ape's remarkably civilized deportment. 'I have seen it sit at table, unfold its napkin, wipe its lips, make use of the spoon and the fork to carry the victuals to its mouth, pour out its drink into a glass, touch glasses when invited, take a cup and saucer and lay them on the table, put in sugar, pour out its tea, leave it to cool before drinking, and all this without any other instigation than the signs or the command of its master, and often of its own accord.'

Buffon goes on to quote one of his acquaintances, M. L. Brosse, who told him about two one-year-old apes he had bought from a Negro: 'Even at that age they sat at table ... made use of their knife, spoon, and fork, both to eat their meat and help themselves; they drank wine and other liquors. We carried them on ship-board, and when they were at table, they made signs to the cabin-boys expressive of their wants ... The male was seasick, and required attendance like a human creature: he was even twice bled in the right arm; and every time afterwards when he found himself indisposed, he showed his arm, as desirous of being relieved by bleeding.'

This pair of apes appears to have come from India. Yet another of Buffon's informants writes as follows of African apes from Sierra Leone: 'If properly fed and instructed when young, they serve as very useful domestics: they usually walk upright, will pound at the mortar, fetch water from the river in a little pitcher, which they carry on their heads; but, if care be not taken to receive the pitcher at their return, they let it fall to the ground, and then, seeing it broken, they begin to lament and cry for the loss.'

The ape's human appearance struck the very earliest travellers. Among them, Marco Polo, who left Venice in the late thirteenth century, describes monkeys he saw in India as having 'such a distinctive appearance that you might take them for men'. He said much the same of those he encountered on his return journey. Visiting Abyssinia – which he called 'Middle India' – he noted that some of the monkeys there 'could almost be said to have the faces of men'.

In classical times, Pliny recorded the tale of a monkey saved by a dolphin. The dolphin swam to the rescue of shipwrecked mariners, carrying them off to safety from their sinking vessel. Among them was a monkey, who was also ferried off astride the dolphin's back, because, so Pliny tells, the dolphin mistook him for a human member of the crew.

This tale of Pliny's is only one more instance of the fact that the monkey's affinity with man has been recognized since time immemorial. And monkeys, in common with other animals, have played their full part in mythology. In at least one Chinese account of the Creation, the disgrace of Monkey is a close parallel to the biblical interpretation of the fall of man, which in turn has much in common with the story of how the ambitious Titans were punished, as told in classical literature.

There was a rock that since the creation of the world had been
worked upon by the pure essences of Heaven and the fine savours
of the Earth, the vigour of sunshine and the grace of moonlight, till
at last it became magically pregnant and one day split open, giving
birth to a stone egg, about as big as a playing ball. Fructified by the
wind, it developed into a stone monkey, complete with every organ
and limb. At once, this monkey learned to climb and run; but its
first act was to make a bow towards each of the four quarters. As it
did so, a steely light darted from this monkey's eyes and flashed as
far as the Palace of the Pole Star. This shaft of light astonished the
Jade Emperor as he sat in the Cloud Palace of the Golden Gates,
in the Treasure Hall of the Holy Mists, surrounded by his fairy
Ministers.

Monkey soon learned many other tricks. He walked and ran,
leaping over the rocks; he drank from the streams, picked wild
flowers and fed off wild fruit. He made friends with the wolf
and the panther and the tiger, the deer and the civet. He even
took to hard liquor, which dimmed the light that shone from his
eyes. Before long, the Stone Monkey elected himself King,
ruling over all the other monkeys and their kindred, the gibbons
and baboons. But it took him a lifetime of fearsome adventure
before he learned wisdom and became a Buddha.

This tale was told by Wu Ch'eng-en, who lived in Kiangsu
province between 1505 and 1580. In his fine translation, the late
Arthur Waley stresses that throughout his earthly pilgrimage
Monkey stands for 'the restless instability of genius'.

The behaviour of apes and monkeys is in many cases so
'human' that it is not surprising they should have been endowed
with human qualities and thought processes. Modern scientists
give innumerable instances of the ape's apparent ability to reason
from cause to effect. 'There is no other animal of which the
baboon reminds one so much as of man.' This was written by
the distinguished South African scientist Eugene Nielen Marais,
whose books *The Soul of the Ape* and *My Friends the Baboons* were
researched and written (in Afrikaans) between the wars. Born in
a farming community near Pretoria in 1872, Marais trained first
in journalism, then took up both medicine and the law (he was
admitted to the bar at the Inner Temple in London). But the

feeling of general loss and isolation which followed the death of his wife drove him to withdraw from human society. He went to live in a remote mountain fastness near Waterberg, where a large group of Chacma baboons ran wild. Thus he became the first man to observe them long and carefully, noting their social habits and inspiring what has become a classic of natural history, *My Friends the Baboons*. It is not a sentimental record of a lonely man driven to seek companionship away from humans, with animals most humans find unattractive. The descriptive gifts of journalism, the discipline and careful observation of the scientist and the accuracy and detail of the lawyer came together to make it, even after forty years, the most eloquent tribute to baboons ever penned. It says in words what the ancient Egyptians tried to convey in their statues. The following examples of baboons behaving 'reasonably' are taken at random from the book.

The first and simplest concerns baboons held in captivity. As Marais tells us, every night a baboon will carry its sleeping-bag to its sleeping-box to use as a cover. He asks, could a dog or a cat, ranked among the most intelligent of animals, thus ensure its own comfort?

Another instance of the ape's outstanding intelligence – and perhaps of something more – concerns a chimpanzee who was reared alongside a tiny marmoset. The two would play happily together for hours on end. But as the chimpanzee grew bigger, and rougher, there was a risk that quite unwittingly he would injure his little playfellow. So Marais decided to keep the two apart until he was free to supervise their play. The marmoset was locked away in a large birdcage. The lock of the cage was elaborate, with a metal chain attached to a pin to secure a slot, which in turn had to be manipulated before it could be pushed out. In addition, the cage was hung from the ceiling, well out of reach. But it was no time before the chimpanzee had mastered the mechanism, after first pulling up a table under the cage and mounting a chair on it to bring itself within reach.

In the second, and more straightforward, case, the chimpanzee was taught to open the complicated lock of a biscuit tin after first fetching the key from a drawer. This, of course, required no more than the intelligence to learn any other trick, such as the routine of begging, coming to heel, fetching, dropping dead, taught to innumerable dogs. But the setting free of the marmoset does suggest some feeling beyond mere intelligence – a dedicated purpose which set the chimpanzee against its master in the cause of its friend.

This case has something in common with what a woman journalist observed at the London Zoo. In a recent article in *The Times* (7.7.84), she tells how she saw a female ape, called Suka, gaze at its keeper with what she says can only be described as pure love. The possible reason was that the keeper and his wife had reared Suka by hand for the first ten months of her life after she had been rejected at birth. But such a tenacious memory in a grown ape which had long since been returned to its natural habitat (in so far as any animal born in captivity can be said to have a natural habitat) suggests something far beyond normal intelligence put to practical purposes.

It may be that further study of the ape will reveal that it has more in common with Homo sapiens than has already been revealed, including those apprehensions and affinities generally described as telepathic, which occasionally show up in human beings.

To quote Marais again, 'We know less about the habits of apes than about those of almost any other land animal. The reason for this is of course the inaccessibility of most apes. In all countries, except Africa, the apes are inhabitants of the densest woods and jungles where it is impossible to keep them in sight for more than a few minutes at a time. Unless one is able to watch animals for days on end uninterruptedly, it is not possible to discover the secrets of their behaviour.'

There is some confirmation of Marais' complaint to be found in the diary that Darwin kept during his voyage round South America in the sailing ship *The Beagle*, which left Devonport (Plymouth) on 27 December 1831. 'The object of the expedition,' Darwin writes, 'was to complete the survey of Patagonia and Tierra del Fuego, commenced under Captain King in 1826 to 1830 – to survey the shores of Chile, Peru, and some of the islands of the Pacific – and to carry a chain of chronometrical measurements round the world.' But Darwin was no mere

cartographer: his real interest lay in collecting further evidence
to support his theory of evolution from the natural fauna. And
as *The Beagle* crossed the Equator and sailed down the Atlantic
coast of the Latin American continent, Darwin and his crew
made many stops to spend days in the tropical forests of Brazil
and elsewhere. The diary lists and describes a big number of
native animals, ranging from deer, armadillos, agoutis (a local
rodent) and vizcachas to the wolf-fox of the Falklands and
including innumerable insects, birds, toads and reptiles. But
there is hardly a mention of apes, apart from a reference to a
monkey shot for the larder.

Since the days of Darwin, and of Eugene Marais, develop-
ments in photography have made the study of wild animals far
easier, as well as far more precise, for a camera can now be
positioned and left to do its work of observation without disturbing the animals' normal routine.

On the other hand, the continuing destruction of the world's
rain forests may soon mean that there won't be much animal life
to observe. The great apes are amongst the most threatened
species and there is not much time left. However, the cause of
conservation is strengthening, and with it the growth of nature
reserves. It is to one of these that a team of researchers went to
study how apes protect themselves from predators. An account
of the expedition led by Dr Hall of Bristol to the nature reserve
at the Cape of Good Hope, where he spent seventy-six days, is
given by the French zoologist Rémy Chauvin in his book on
animal societies. The problem that Dr Hall and his colleagues
set out to solve concerned the security system which apes had
long been thought to set up. As Chauvin puts it, 'Naturalists
have always observed the presence of sentinels among baboons.
There are at least two or three situations when the behaviour of
the guards can be observed at leisure: when the presence of a
man is detected by the baboons in the early morning, just as they
are coming down from the tree-tops where they have spent the
night; when the observers have already been noticed, but a
sudden mist has hidden them from view; or lastly when a
neighbouring tribe trespasses on their territory.'

However, there had been numerous reports of the alleged

defence system breaking down – big-game hunters, for instance, had found themselves suddenly in the midst of a tribe of baboons. Such incidents were too well authenticated not to put into question the whole theory of the apes' early warning system. This is what Hall and his colleagues went to find out, but the evidence they brought back was inconclusive. They saw sentinels, chosen from among the biggest males, apparently standing guard; they heard the young of the tribe who seemed to have been set to patrol the borders of the colony's territory and heard them give shrill cries of alarm. But the big apes appeared to ignore their calls: not once were they heard to utter the piercing yell which alerts the tribe to approaching danger. Hall's findings were no doubt a disappointment for scientists, but they do suggest that the apes of the Cape of Good Hope were well aware that no danger could come to them. Perhaps they were merely putting on a show for their human visitors?

That apes and monkeys get up to their tricks is well known. The Swedish doctor Axel Munthe, whose love of animals led him to take a lot of time off from his fashionable Paris clientele to visit his friends at the zoo, tells of an aged baboon called Jules who had him taped. When Munthe arrived at the Jardin des Plantes, Jules would rub his tummy and roll his eyes about to express extremes of pain. To indicate his loss of appetite, he would regretfully decline the apple offered to him. Without prompting, he would stick out his tongue for examination. Then, quick as lightning, he would snatch from Munthe's pocket the bananas he knew were always there and, leaping to the top bars of his cage, would sit eating and rejoicing at the success of his ploy. This routine was, of course, a double-take – and Jules may well have known it, but he continued to cash in on his doctor's good nature.

Not all visitors to the zoo share Munthe's liking for baboons – they may think the baboon a very primitive and unattractive animal, or they do not like the animal's glazed and vividly coloured buttocks, which seem to them so ugly but which are in fact part of its means of attracting a mate. The baboon has none of the sense of mischief (or so it seems at first) of certain types of monkey, with their ceaseless curiosity; nor the impressive, almost terrifying, bulk of the gorilla. Other people in other countries and periods have taken an altogether different view of them, sensing a mystery in their behaviour and impressed by their perception and intelligence.

Throughout Asia and Africa, the baboon has been worshipped in many guises. Baboons have been deemed to enjoy the special favour and protection of the gods, and sometimes worshipped as gods themselves. The mummified remains of baboons of the Hamadryad variety found today in Ethiopia, Sudan and some parts of the Middle East show that they were buried with all the honours accorded to rulers, priests and noblemen. In Ancient Egypt, the baboon god Thoth had the important role of weighing the souls of the dead. Berlin's State museum has an impressive statue showing a colossal baboon standing behind a man, as though to protect him. Records show that the Egyptians actually domesticated baboons, training them to do useful jobs about the house and farm, sharing their homes with the animals as though they were equals – or superiors, for their place in religion was very important. In their role as super-watchdogs, as the Berlin statue implies, they would certainly have been effective; they are strong, fearless and intelligent, unlikely to transfer their allegiance from an accepted master to a total stranger! The male baboon has a formidable bite, and zoo-keepers maintain that baboons are frequently more dangerous than lions and tigers.

But the Swiss psychiatrist Carl Gustav Jung (1875-1961), who was Freud's rival in founding analytical psychology, was impressed with the spiritual air of baboons during his travels in Kenya and Uganda in the early 1920s.

Near my observation point was a high cliff inhabited by big baboons. Every morning they sat quietly, almost motionless, on the ridge of the cliff facing the sun, whereas throughout the rest of the day they ranged noisily through the forest, screeching and chattering. Like me, they seemed to be waiting for the sunrise. They reminded me of the great baboons of the temple of Abu Simbel in Egypt, which perform the gesture of adoration. They tell the same story: for untold ages men have worshipped the great god who redeems the world by rising out of the darkness as a radiant light in the heavens.

At that time I understood that within the soul from its primordial beginnings there has been a desire for light and an irrepressible urge to rise out of the primal darkness. . . . There is sadness in the animals' eyes, and we never know whether that sadness is bound up with the soul of the animal or is a poignant message which speaks to us out of that still unconscious existence.

The magnificent temple of Abu Simbel to which Jung refers is crowned by a frieze of baboons, which was caught by the first rays of the rising sun. The sort of spectacle he observed when the baboons sat patiently waiting for the sun to shine on them may well have given rise to the idea, prevalent in ancient Egypt, that the baboons were sun-worshippers and, as such in those days, sacred.

In modern times, it is Marais who reminds that the baboon, for all its unprepossessing aspect and ungainly ways, fully deserves the interest and respect of mankind.

Marais observed a type of 'communism' by which a new-born babe is protected by its father and mother exclusively after birth but, as soon as it can walk, is handled and fondled by all the large members of the group. He noted the fearlessness and cunning with which the baboons would attack a leopard: yet they would use caution in approaching a python, even preferring to abandon one of their number to its deadly clutches rather than endanger the whole troop. Again and again he observed behaviour which, in his own words, was 'ridiculously human'. For example, a new-born baboon becomes the centre of interest, as at a human family gathering, the baboons forming a small company and passing the baby from hand to hand after an examination. 'It is almost as if you could hear the mother murmur to herself, "Yes, have a good look, you have never seen such a baby before."'

Why should there be some secret understanding, some sort of affinity, between baboons and men? Is there, buried deep down in the subconscious, some knowledge of a common ancestry? Can baboons read the thoughts of human beings, knowing which mean harm and which are friends? A troop of baboons would let Marais come very near and attempt no harm; but should any or one of the baby baboons show the slightest fear or repulsion, a male would advance, meaning business, for in their protection of their young they are utterly altruistic and fear nothing. A human 'friend' ceases to be a friend if, for whatever reason or no reason at all, a young baboon is made unhappy by human nearness of presence. Their grief, too, is very similar in its manifestations, and its causes, to that experienced by human beings. Marais refers to the 'terrible, blood-freezing cry of woe from the baboons – persistent and heart-rending' which sounded to his ears 'more moving than even the cry of mourning of human beings . . . a purely emotional sound more or less similar to the inarticulate groaning and sighing by which the deepest anguish of the human heart finds speechless expression'.

On going to the sleeping-place of the baboons to find out what was distressing them, he discovered, below the sheer rock face on the floor of the narrow gorge, the corpses of eight young baboons, just weaned, which had died during the night and had been cast out, as baboons do with their dead. Normally with lower animals, it would have been hazardous to attempt to remove the babies, but the baboons made no protest as Marais and his companions took them away. At this point, Marais experienced what he believed was an extraordinary attempt by one of the baboons to communicate something to him:

> . . . one unfortunate mother followed almost on our heels with all kinds of begging sounds, and here we discovered something wonderful. It was not for the return of her child that she was begging, for when we placed all the bodies on the ground in front of her, (we could not distinguish her infant from the others) she touched, in a most moving way, her own child with her lips. But it was only for a few seconds. She did not try to pick up the babe or take away the body. And then almost at once she sat with her arms stretched out to us continuously and continued her begging. What did she want? Obviously not the return of her dead infant. But she did want something which, to her dim intelligence, we alone were able to give her. She wanted exactly what the seven large males, who had visited us so unexpectedly the previous evening, had wanted – our help to ward off the approaching death from the infants – that approaching death of which, in all probability, they had become aware the previous evening. And the mother wanted from us the revival of her child. . . .

Marais had wondered, on the previous evening, why seven males had unexpectedly visited them. He concluded that they had come for help, just as the mother was now begging them to bring her infant back to life. Marais encountered much proof that advanced 'thinking' of this kind was not at all improbable. The mother followed them back to their huts, 'and waited a long time before hope deserted her'.

Although baboons are to be found in zoos throughout the world, attempts to raise a baboon as one of a human family are rare. But Julie Macdonald, an American sculptor, had often kept animals of all sorts and used them as models. 'In recent years,' she relates, with justifiable pride, in *Almost Human*, 'my children and I, who have shared our home with wild animals, have raised a Hamadryad baboon as a member of the family.' Keeping notes of its daily activities, its attitude to people and to other animals, she became conscious of 'the development of a strong emotional bond between foster parent and adopted animal' which 'serves to erase the contrived line of demarcation between the observer and the observed'. The baboon, a female, was named Abu, after the temple of Abu Simbel.

Like some humans, Abu had an instinctive fear of solitude and would scream when left alone. When she was picked up, she would throw her arms around Mrs Macdonald and hug her with all her might. She would drive in the car with the family and dined at table with them with 'surprising restraint and daintiness of manners'. Like a child, she could have tantrums and throw things about – with well-directed aim. During a domestic upheaval in the Macdonald home, Julie was depressed: as a result, Abu's appetite diminished. But as the pall of depression rose and the emotional atmosphere cleared, Abu's spirits rose too.

Since baboons are able to *think* – to reason out problems and find a practical answer, we may justifiably consider every baboon as having its own personality, or psyche. The most outstanding authenticated case of a 'thinking' baboon is that of Chacma Jack, who became a signalman at Uitenhage Railway Station in the eastern province of the Cape of Good Hope. His master found that running from his hut to the signals (quite a short distance) was fatiguing, for he had lost both legs in a railway accident and walked on poles affixed to his stumps. Why should he stomp there and back if his baboon could do it? So he taught the baboon how to pull the appropriate levers to work the signals for the approaching trains. The baboon learned the name of each lever, and his master had only to tell him which one to pull and he would race to do it, with relish and invariable accuracy!

Chacma Jack was inseparable from his master, and together they would ride home on a trolley, Jack getting out to push when the gradient was too steep. Sad to relate, this intelligent and faithful baboon met his death at the hands of a drunkard, who killed him with a blow on the head.

It is often in death that the primates come nearest to us human beings. Axel Munthe recounts, in moving detail, the death of another of his friends, Jack the gorilla. They had known each other a good many years when Jack evinced the symptoms of the pulmonary disease which had carried off so many of the doctor's patients in the paupers' ward of the Salle Sainte-Claire. Jack's symptoms were all too recognizable – the violent coughing which at last brought on a slight haemorrhage of the lungs, the loss of appetite, the fever and, towards the end, the heavy irregular respiration and the phlegm rattling in the throat. 'One morning,' Munthe says, 'I found him lying on his bed with the blanket pulled over his head, just as my patients in the Salle Sainte-Claire used to lie, when they were tired to death and sick of everything . . . Presently a sharp fit of coughing shook his whole body. He sat up in his bed and put his two hands to his temples in a gesture of despair. The whole expression of his face had changed. He had cast off his animal disguise and become a dying human being.'

After Jack died, his body was handed over to the scientists. His skeleton, with its large brain pan, was preserved, standing erect in a Paris museum, Munthe tells us. He asks: 'But is that all?'

12
Animals as Gods – The Mystic Link

In the Louvre Museum in Paris is a crocodile mummified thousands of years ago in ancient Egypt. The care with which it has been embalmed and the intricate craftsmanship of its tight, intertwined linen swathings are a reminder of the awe and reverence with which this highly dangerous creature was once regarded. Once *Crocodilus Niloticus* was common to the Nile, Egypt's vital artery which alone made irrigation and civilization possible. Probably the crocodiles were regarded as guardians appointed by the gods to protect the river.

Although the crocodile was hunted, it was considered sacred to the god Sebek, the crocodile divinity. Sometimes Sebek is shown as a man with the head of a crocodile, or merely as a crocodile. This representation of animals as gods, or of gods which are a combination of animals and men, is very common in most ancient religions. A papyrus in Turin Museum shows a crocodile playing a lute.

It was not merely the guardianship of the swamps, or of the Nile, which earned crocodiles the worship of Egyptians. The crocodiles' strength and cunning, their habit of floating with only their noses and eyes showing, or on their backs looking like drifting logs, and their occasional recourse to man-eating, were considered proof of extra-human intelligence, while the fact that they were seen to leave the river to deposit their eggs on the banks was linked in the minds of Egyptians with an old legend of creation, according to which the Demiurge appeared from beneath the dark immensity of the waters and created the world. Throughout the province of Fayyum the crocodile was worshipped as a protector, yet it was execrated in other parts because Set, murderer of the god Osiris, was supposed to have hidden in the body of a crocodile to escape punishment.

Was this terrifying creature ever the *friend* of man? The Greek historian Diodorus Siculus describes how King Menes, founder of the First Dynasty, was attached by hunting dogs and saved by a crocodile, on whose back he was carried to safety across Lake Maeris.

The helpful crocodile reappears among early Christianity's Desert Fathers. The Abbot Helenus refused to accept his monks' excuse that they could not celebrate Mass because their priest was unable to cross the crocodile-infested river. Setting out to fetch the recalcitrant priest, Helenus reached the river's edge where 'the crocodile at once took him upon its back and ferried him over to the opposite bank'. On the return journey, accompanied this time by the priest, all Helenus had to do was to summon the crocodile to carry them back.

Helen Waddell, who tells the story, adds another instance – that of St Pachmore, Abbot of Tabenne, who had the local crocodiles at his call. She adds to his legend that he had so much trust in God 'that many a time he trod on snakes and scorpions, and passed unhurt through them'. Other powers attributed to the crocodile are less easy to judge for good or evil. The Egyptologist Sir Wallis Budge, quoting from ancient texts, reveals that the crocodile was reputed to carry off women and 'unite' with them: 'He is the sower of seed, who carries off wives from their husbands to the place which pleases him, according to the inclination of his heart.'

Even in the Book of Job, one of the oldest records in the world, there is a clear reference to the crocodile, since the words could apply to no other denizen of the water: 'Canst thou draw Leviathan with a hook? Or his tongue with a chord, which thou lettest down? . . . Lay thy hand upon him, remember the battle, do no more.'

One may wonder indeed how it was that an animal so dangerous to hunt, and whose stealth made it often impossible to avoid, should have attracted so much adulation – the mummified crocodile in the Louvre Museum is proof that it was regarded as likely to achieve, and to be as worthy of, immortality as man himself. All those thousands of years ago, the ancient Egyptians were among the first to recognize that animals had a special role in the scheme of things, possessing qualities and capacities equal to, and often superior to, those of man. Animals were not only a link between gods and men but were often gods themselves.

The cat, still one of the world's most popular pets, established its importance and popularity thousands of years ago. For century after century it has been the friend of man, but its self-containedness and aura of mysterious detachment secured for it a special place in Egyptian religion. A cat goddess was a national divinity a thousand years before Christ, and a city, Bubastis, was named in her honour. The ruins of Tell Basta, including the site of a temple mentioned by Herodotus, 'the father of history', are all that remain of the splendour of the cat-capital. The temple, once one of the finest in Egypt, attracted hundreds of thousands of pilgrims to its huge annual festivals, where music and dancing, feasting and drinking, continued for days. There were masques and processions and innumerable consecrations of statues of cats. People came considerable distances to attend these celebrations, usually by barge, and many a weeping family went to the consecrated sanctuary to bury their mummified cats with elaborate ceremony. Bast (or Bubastis or Bastet) was a benign goddess who combined wisdom with tolerance, and there was neither limit nor inhibition in the festivities held in her honour; Herodotus described them frankly as riotous.

The goddess's mild and playful disposition was based on what the Egyptians had observed of their domestic cats – the combination of mischief and dignified aloofness, of some inborn but secret wisdom. Bubastis was credited with protecting people from plagues and evil spirits. A statue in Berlin shows a cat-headed goddess holding a sistrum (a musical instrument of ancient Egypt consisting of a metal rattle) in her right hand and a 'lion aegis' (pectoral surmounted by the head of a lioness). A basket hangs from her left arm.

So revered were cats in ancient Egypt that to kill one was the most heinous of crimes, attracting the most condign punishment, even death. If a fire occurred, the first concern of those who fought it was to save the lives of any cats which might be on the premises, in unquestioned priority over any human inhabitants.

The British Museum in London possesses one of the most extraordinary and impressive examples of Egyptian artists investing a cat with dignity and mystery. The Gayer-Anderson cat indeed looks like a cat – sleepy, feline and strong – but it also looks, as was clearly intended by the artist, *godlike*. It exudes an extraordinary impression of mystical power. Around its neck is an impression of the *utchat*, the all-seeing eye of Horus. The eye recesses are deep and so ably sculpted that the lighting effect gives the impression that the eyes are there – alert, penetrating. In the course of thousands of years of Egyptian artistic achievement innumerable portraits of cats have been executed, sometimes as statues, frequently in tombs and on sarcophagi, occasionally in cameo or intaglio on rings, necklaces and ornaments – and ancient papyri contain innumerable references.

In their own way, cats have served mankind well, not merely as pets but as useful and protective predators keeping down the number of rodents which spread disease and caused widespread famine by menacing corn stores. But no such practical consideration can have accounted solely for the extreme veneration in which the Egyptians held them. To them, cats were sacred.

It has been said that the ancient Egyptians were not only the most religious, but the most superstitious people the world has ever known. Given the immense variety of religions which have existed and exist still, I know of no sound criterion by which such a generalization can be justified. Even so, it is unarguable that the ancient Egyptians worshipped a complex immensity of gods and maintained in their daily lives a number of elaborate and mandatory religious rituals. The extent to which animals figure in their hierarchy of gods has no parallel in any other period or country, even allowing for the fact that animal gods figure prominently in the cultural development of many other countries.

Apis the bull god was maintained in splendour in a temple specially built for him at Memphis, in northern Egypt, the administrative and artistic centre of Lower Egypt, on the Nile. The Temple contained extensive walks and courts for his amusement. At a fixed hour each day the live bull-god was led out to disport himself before a crowd of devout onlookers. His birthday, which was celebrated every year, was a day of rejoicing for the whole of Egypt. His death was the occasion of public mourning which ended only when another sacred bull had been discovered to succeed him. Apis was presumed to be the product of a virgin birth – a heifer had been fecundated by heavenly fire, so it was believed, a disguise assumed by Ptah, one of the four great gods credited with the creation of the world.

The sacred bulls were identified by priests, who looked for certain markings as proof that they were the reincarnation of Ptah. Once authenticated, the animals could look forward to a life of bullish ease, and woe betide any visitor to the temple who dared to show amusement or disrespect when the bull was let loose in the temple courtyard, whatever its antics or activities might be. The worship of bulls by the Egyptians provoked and irritated the conquering Persians, who on two occasions killed the sacred bull. These acts of sacrilege aroused feelings of such intense grief and outrage that the priests announced that Ptah had appeared amongst them yet again, being immortal, bearing the unique and unmistakable markings of identity. There was universal relief and rejoicing at the announcement.

The funeral ceremony for a bull was comparable with that accorded a war hero nowadays, such as the funeral of Field-Marshal Montgomery of Alamein. Like kings and important personages, they were buried in monolithic granite or stone coffins (sarcophagi), and excavations in early Victorian times at Sakkara unearthed a tremendous network of underground caverns where the sacred bulls were buried.

The cult of Mithras, the god of light and wisdom among the Persians, was introduced to Rome, where it flourished and spread throughout the empire – within recent years, in the course of excavations for a new building, a Mithraic temple was uncovered in the City of London. In the final struggle between Paganism and Christianity, it exercised a powerful attraction. At this stage, Mithraism, which had begun as sun worship, was centred round the bull. Witness the fine bulls' heads which crown columns preserved in the Louvre from the palace of Artaxerxes II at Suma. The god Mithras himself is commonly represented throughout the Hellenic world as a handsome youth, kneeling on a bull and cutting its throat. In doing do, he is carrying out a fertility rite, as is shown by the luxuriant vegetation of all kinds which springs up as blood flows from the wound. The most striking ceremony of the Mithraic cult was the blood baptism, called Taurobolium.

The bull cult was common to other countries. It was enormously important in Crete, where the Greek legends of the Minotaur, half-bull, half-man, originated. Cretan sports centred round the highly dangerous game of grabbing the bull by the horns, vaulting over his back and generally challenging the bull's strength and skill. Friezes recovered from the Palace of Knossos, of the late Minoan period, around 1500 BC, show this sport being practised and, one hopes, enjoyed – certainly by the spectators. But whereas bulls were sacrificed in Crete as well as being venerated, to kill a sacred cow in India would be tantamount to killing a man. Even in the third century before Christ, the Emperor Asoka proclaimed throughout his empire that the ritual killing of animals must stop and that animal life must be treated with reverence. The modern world did not invent animal sanctuaries. The Emperor Asoka and many other rulers formed closed compounds – something which we would consider a cross between a national park and a zoo – where species of every kind, including birds, could move free of menace from the hunter or trapper. Buddhism brought with it a message of love, a sense of the indivisibility of nature, and the interdependence of men and animals.

Even before then (before the sixth century BC) the close relationship between animals and men was a basic fact of existence; by his labour alone man could not survive. To kill a cow was not only a crime as heinous as murder but entailed for so foolhardy a culprit the Gilbertian punishment of being forced to wear the skin of the animal he had killed, of joining the herd and living with it and being fed on nothing but barley for months.

All in all, the anthropomorphic gods (those conceived as having human form or some semblance of it) are vastly outnumbered by those gods which are either animals or zoomorphic (part human, part animal). From country to country, from period to period, the conviction that animals possessed marvellous and mystical powers has been taken almost for granted, so that, in the visualization of gods, animals took precedence over men. The lion, monkey, ape, jackal, snake, dog – even the scorpion and the frog – have all in their time been deified.

The dolphin, which as a sea animal is an oddity in itself, was the subject of worship in ancient Crete. From there its cult spread to Mainland Greece – indeed, it was held that Apollo had assumed the shape of a dolphin to guide storm-tossed mariners safely into harbour, landing at Crissa, south-west of Delphi. The whole region became sacred to Apollo: on his birthday, by tradition 17 April, a Delphic festival was held to mark the coming of calmer seas and implore his continued protection of seafarers.

The Greeks also believed that Apollo's son, Icadius, was saved by a dolphin when he was shipwrecked near Lycia. The dolphin carried him on his back and landed him near Mount Parnassus where in gratitude he founded another shrine sacred to his father, which became celebrated as the seat of Apollo and the Muses.

Grecian coins show a man riding on a dolphin. In his *Natural History*, Pliny gives us the tale of a dolphin who regularly ferried a boy across 'the broad arm of the sea' to school at Puteoli. Pliny adds, 'There is no end of examples in his kind: Amphilocians and Tarentines testify as much, as touching dolphins which have been enamoured of little boys.'

This leads Pliny to believe in the famous legend of Arion, 'a notable musician and player of the harp' who lived about 625 BC at the Court of Corinth. On one occasion he went from there to Sicily to take part in a musical contest. He won the prize and, laden with gifts, took ship for home. But the sailors, who coveted his treasures, decided to kill him and pretend he had been lost at sea. However, they granted him a last request – to play once more on his cithara. Having invoked the gods, he threw himself into the sea. Then the song-loving dolphins, who had been following the ship, rose out of the water, making noises of pleasure and cavorting with delight as if to acclaim the musician. One of them actually took Arion upon its back and swam him to safety. Eventually he reached Corinth, just as the murderous sailors landed with their tale of the lost passenger. Arion told his tale to his protector, the tyrant Periander; the sailors were made to confess their guilt and received their just deserts.

The fables about dolphins may well not have been fables at all, but based on fact. And the facts about dolphins, whether people were right to think of them as goods or not, suggest that they were more worthy of worship than the cruel and greedy emperors who ascribed divinity to themselves to strengthen their rule and their hold upon the minds of their subject peoples; more worthy, too, than many of the anthropomorphic gods, often credited with sharing the vices and cruelties of men.

Snakes feature prominently in magic and religion. Crete had its snake-goddess, while Nebti, the Egyptian snake-goddess, is often shown near representations of Pharaoh as a protection against his enemies.

Birds impressed by their flight, their speed, their self-sufficiency. Horus was a falcon god in ancient Egypt. The Assyrian god Ningirsu was depicted as an eagle. In Slavonic folklore, a power called the Volga could assume numerous forms, including that of a hawk. Mont, the Egyptian god, sometimes had the head of a hawk; at others he was shown with a bull's. Rather oddly, the Egyptian goddess charged with the protection of the young in childbirth was Nekhebet, often depicted in the form of a vulture – in modern times one of the least-loved birds.

The crow was regarded in many periods as a messenger of death or harbinger of misfortune; a number are said to have flown around Cicero's head on the day he was murdered, and crows were said to possess magical powers, including the gift of prophecy. It has been suggested that this may have something to do with the crow's cry of '*cras*' – the Latin word for 'tomorrow'.

13

Birds as Gods

Aviation is one of the more recent skills and sciences, and for most of man's evolution the heavens have been regarded as remote and unfathomable, so much so that even in ancient Greece Mount Olympus was considered the abode of the gods. It was observed with awe that birds could soar with ease to great heights, often disappearing entirely from view, as though heaven itself was their home. From the recognition of their freedom in regions that were forbidden to man, it is easy to imagine how it was that birds came to be regarded as gods, exercising an active role in the shaping of man's destiny.

Thus the Egyptian sun-god Horus was represented as either a falcon or a falcon-headed man. 'Hor' meant 'sky', which, in Egyptian hieroglyphs, was represented by the standing figure of a falcon; it was connected with another symbol meaning 'upper' – in effect, a high-flyer, which, of course, the bird is. In early Egyptian writings one of the most usual symbols of divinity was a falcon on its perch, whilst in later dynasties it represented the king, who was regarded as all-powerful and descended from the gods. The falcon-headed god enjoyed an immense following in many dynasties, his image being commonly carried as a totem. At Buto and El Kab, in the two primeval kingdoms of Upper and Lower Egypt, hawk gods were the presiding deities of the royal quarters of Poi and Nekhen.

One of the principal festivals was devoted to the worship of Horus, and over the centuries a whole variety of hawk and falcon gods appeared. Originally, as I have said, Horus was a sky-god, but the winged solar disc, so favourite an emblem of old Egypt even today, is really a variation of Horus – Hor or Beht. Harmakhis or Hor of the Horizon, the sun-god of Heliopolis, was another variation; so was Har-Messen, whose sacred animal was the lion. The falcon was more commonly the bird sacred to Horus, but the immense numbers of mummified hawks, sparrow-hawks and kestrels discovered suggest that these birds too were held sacred. Hawks were also held in high esteem by the Turks – killing a hawk was punished by death. Priests and augurs examined their swift flight to foretell future events. And incidentally hawks may have served a useful purpose, for they were believed to destroy snakes and scorpions.

Of the family of predatory birds, the eagle was king, a royal bird sacred to Jupiter. The Roman legions adopted the eagle as their mascot; it also figured on the ensigns of Babylonic, Persian and Egyptian rulers. In Rome, the custom of letting an eagle fly from the funeral pyre of a deceased emperor signified that the emperor's soul was ascending into the realms beyond.

The eagle as a symbol of re-incarnation appears in the Bible: where the Psalms say 'Thy youth is renewed like the eagle's', the reference is to the belief that every ten years the eagle soars into the sky and into the flaming sun itself, then plunges into the sea where it moults and re-emerges with new plumage and new life. The cherubs referred to in the Bible in the description of King Solomon's temple have eagles' wings. Their task was to protect the throne or chariot of the god Yahweh and the Ark of the Tabernacle. Since then, in innumerable pictures and carvings, they are depicted as sacred guardians. In this sense, they themselves were considered sacred, and objects bearing their representation were treated with the greatest reverence. In the modern Church, the lectern which bears the Holy Book is often in the shape of an eagle.

In due course the eagle was adopted by many countries as their emblem. The two-headed eagle as an emblem dates from 1472, when the Tsar of Russia married a niece of Constantine XIV, the last Emperor of Byzantium. The two heads represent the Eastern (Byzantine) Empire and the Western (Roman) Empire. The adoption by Germany, at the time of Charlemagne, of the two-headed eagle as a symbol of the Kaiser had a somewhat similar purpose. The eagle was also one of several Napoleonic devices; the Emperor's son was known as *'l'Aiglon'* – the Eaglet. The United States' crest is also an eagle. So is Poland's.

There are still vestigial reminders of the god-like nature once ascribed to eagles. The Ostyaks of Siberia regarded as holy any tree in which an eagle built its nest for several years in succession, and would spare both birds and tree because of it. It was long, long afterwards that Britain had to take special measures to protect the vanishing species of golden eagle. The might and mysticism of the eagle persisted even into modern times in the superstition that for two people to eat one eagle's egg boiled would keep witches away. However, one would need to be very frightened of witches to try to snatch an egg from an eagle's nest.

Still in the realms of magic, there is a close link, and an extended one, between the mythical phoenix and the eagle. The Greek historian Herodotus, who held that the phoenix died and was revived every 500 years, described it as a bird with red-golden feathers. The Roman Tacitus says it made an appearance in Egypt in AD 34. Christianity adopted the legend of the phoenix, making it into a symbol both of Christ's resurrection and of man's eventual resurrection after the Fall. Kevin Crossley-Holland has translated this account of the bird's death and renewal from the work of an anonymous Anglo-Saxon poet:

Then the bird is burnt
With its nest in the fire's fierce embrace.
The funeral pyre is kindled. Fire engulfs the nest of the sad phoenix; fast and furious the yellow flames flicker and the age-old bird is burnt. Thus fire falls on the frail body; the life, the spirit of the fated one leaves on a journey. Yet, in due time, life is restored to him. . . . First it is like an eaglet, a fair fledgling; but it increases further, in great joy, until it is like an eagle come to maturity; and after that beautifully adorned with brilliant plumage it is as it was in the beginning.

That homely and useful bird the goose was considered sacred in Rome, and the familiar legend of how the sacred geese saved the Capitol commemorates the gratitude of its inhabitants. According to this, when the Gauls were invading Rome, they crept so silently, in single file, up the hill, that the first man to arrive was not even challenged; but while he was going over the ramparts, the sacred geese broke out into so noisy a cacophony that the garrison was awakened – just in time.

There can hardly be a sillier phrase than 'silly as a goose' – as Dr Johnson puts it in his Dictionary definition of the goose, 'A large waterfowl proverbially noted, I know not why, for foolishness.' Their intelligence and their seeming affection for human beings earned them high respect in ancient times. Their sense of hearing, seeing and smelling is unusually acute. The goose was held by the Romans to be sacred to Juno (Hera), a moon goddess, goddess of childbirth, consort of the god Jupiter and protector of the Roman people. As Jupiter is king of the gods, so Juno is queen of the heavens. Her particular function is to watch over the female sex; she is goddess of womanhood. In Rome, she was also goddess of finance and, as Juno Moneta, had a temple in the Capitoline Hill.

There are more cogent reasons for the awe and respect in which geese were held by the Romans.

A friend of mine, recently on holiday in Barcelona, wandered into the cathedral cloisters and was astonished to find geese – white geese – waddling about, some from and some to a pool. Curious as to the historical reasons for this, she found a reference in H. V. Morton's *A Stranger in Spain*:

> I wandered into the magnificent cloisters where geese have been kept for centuries. The fat birds, as white as snow against the ancient stones, swim in little ponds arranged in the angle of the cloister, or waddle slowly, turning a reflective eye to those who venture to offer scraps of bread to them. They call them the Capitoline Geese. No one could tell me why or explain the origin of this custom. Perhaps their remote predecessors were Roman geese who lived on the same spot when Barcelona was Colonia Faventia Julia Augusta Pia Barcino.

Dame Rose Macaulay, the English novelist (1881-1958) in *Fabled Shore* refers to the birds as 'Capitoline Geese'. The Barcelona geese are a reminder of the tradition that when the Gauls invaded Rome in 390 BC, a detachment in single file crept stealthily up the hill of the Capitol, actually reaching the top without being challenged. But the first man, on stepping over the rampart, disturbed the sacred geese, whose cackling awoke the garrison. Marcus Manlius rushed to the wall, throwing the intruder over the precipice, while the alerted garrison dealt summarily with the rest. To commemorate the event the Romans carried a golden gooše in procession to the Capitol every year.

Edward Stanley, Bishop of Norwich and a Fellow of the Royal Society in Victorian times, quotes a touching story related by Pliny the Elder, the Roman scholar and naturalist: 'A person named Lacydes, a philosopher, had a Goose which took so strong a fancy to him, that it would never willingly leave him by night or day – wherever he went the Goose was his companion; if he went abroad and walked in the public streets, the bird followed him, and, in his own house, always forced itself into his presence. The philosopher, struck with this constant and strange attachment, seems to have considered it as in some way or other connected with religious feelings, and accordingly, when at last he died, he was at the expense of bestowing upon it a magnificent funeral.'

But, as the great humanist printer Charles Estienne (1504-64) wrote, the goose and the favourite household pet, the dog, had much in common: 'Their watch and warde is good and gainfull, being indeed better than that of the dogge, as hatch beene shewed long agoe by the geese of the Capitoll in Rome.'

It is interesting to note that Buddha, who was incarnated in many forms, re-appeared as seven different birds, one of them a goose; his other incarnations included two forms of sea-life and seven different species of land animals.

The mystic link between geese and gods had something to do with the fact that the arrival of flocks of geese was a signal for the coming of spring. Spring was a rebirth, a season of renewal and fertility. Thus the goose became symbolic of life and in special favour with the gods.

Sometimes the religious associations were not so lucky for the goose itself: it was sacrificed at Swedish funerals, and in autumn to the German god Odin. (Odin was the Scandinavian name for the god which the Anglo-Saxons called Woden; the day of the week which we nowadays call Wednesday is a derivation from Woden's Day.) In Germany the town of Cologne once paid homage to a goose goddess. The inhabitants of the Isle of Rhodes welcomed the arrival of geese with a song.

In many countries and at different times the goose was assumed to carry gods to their destinations – the Japanese goddess Kosenko is borne aloft on a goose; so too was the goddess of love, Aphrodite; Brahma, in Hinduism the creator of the universe, rides through the heavens on a gander.

In folklore and mythology, as in religion, one of the most striking things is the persistence of imagery and broadly similar ideas, even between peoples who had no contact with each other and in cultures quite isolated from other cultures. This is particularly true of birds as divinities, or birds as messengers of companions of the gods.

The crow, as *Brewer's Dictionary of Phrase and Fable* puts it, 'symbolises contention, discord and strife'. The ravens, of the crow family, owe part of their sinister reputation to their odious habit of picking out the eyes of a corpse – as the wicked are warned in Proverbs. Its colour, black, invested the raven with ideas of darkness, oblivion and death. Ravens are said to have foretold the death of Alexander the Great by circling round his victorious forces as they entered Babylon, while King Marres of Egypt was reputed to send messages by means of a crow. In ancient Greece the raven was an attendant of Apollo. The Norse people believed that their god Odin possessed two ravens, which flew around all day collecting information. In the evening they would perch upon his shoulders, giving him the latest news they had gathered – a highly economical form of secret service.

In both the Old and the New Testaments the raven figures frequently, and in Christian history. The ravens fed Elijah. St Benedict is often depicted with a raven at his feet. It was a raven which brought St Paul the Hermit a loaf of bread. The keeping of ravens at the Tower of London is a strange tradition, when one comes to think of it, for it is assumed that bad luck will result if they leave the place. Yet the building itself has so sinister a history that, far from relieving the all-pervading gloom of the place, some think that the presence of the ravens heightens it.

Even today many superstitions about ravens linger on. In parts of Britain – and in many other countries too – the raven's croak is held to be a sign of danger or death. But a more genial legend persists in the Welsh superstition that if a blind person is kind to a raven his sight will be restored. In Cornwall the superstition persists that the soul of King Arthur took the form of a raven, for which reason one of the species could never be shot. In Brazil, a similar belief exists – it is held that the human soul can inhabit the body of a raven.

One curious feature of the behaviour of crows is their seeming capacity to hold 'courts' at which, by numerous accounts, they pass judgement and carry out summary execution, of such of their numbers as, for some mysterious reason, they consider deserving of it. As Edward Stanley, the Victorian naturalist, put it:

> In the Northern part of Scotland, and in the Faroe Islands, extraordinary meetings of crows are known to occur. They collect in great numbers, as if they had all been summoned, for the occasion; a few of the flock sit with drooping heads, and the others seem as grave as judges, while others again are exceedingly active and noisy: in the course of about an hour they disperse and it is not uncommon, after they have flown away, to find one or two left dead on the spot. Another writer (in Dr Edmonston's *Shetland Isles*), says that these meetings will sometimes continue for a day or two, before the object, whatever it may be, is completed. Crows continue to arrive from all quarters during the season. As soon as they have all arrived, a very general noise ensues, and, shortly after, the whole fall upon one or two individuals, and put them to death: when this execution has been performed, they quietly disperse.

The gentle and cooing dove, in modern times and for centuries in Christian times, has symbolized the human soul. In religious art it is often seen emerging from the mouths of saints. It also – and primarily – represents the Holy Ghost (Spirit), and the seven rays that emanate from it, as depicted in so much religious art and sculpture, represent the seven gifts of the Holy Ghost. St David appears with a dove on his shoulders; St Gregory is in company with a dove. Noah sent forth three birds to see if the floods had subsided, but it was the dove that returned with the proof that God's vengeance had eased and the floods ended.

Doves have been domesticated for thousands of years and

feature in ancient art – in Egyptian tomb paintings, for instance – as much as in recent times. In classical mythology the dove became associated with Aphrodite, the Greek goddess of love and beauty. In the vegetable kingdom, the myrtle, the rose, the apple and poppy are sacred to her. Among animals, the sparrow, the swan, the swallow and the dove are often shown drawing her chariot or carrying messages for her. Her son Eros (or Cupid), who is her constant companion, has his bird-like attributes: he is represented with golden wings and fluttering about like a bird.

In her Roman form, Aphrodite becomes Venus. Her worship was widespread and, as goddess of spring, the month of April was sacred to her. The association of doves with the goddess of love is not difficult to understand, since, to the superficial observer at least, they seem always to be billing and cooing and, like other birds, they reproduce rapidly.

The dove as a symbol of peace goes back to the time when it returned to the Ark carrying the olive branch. Since then, it has generally been regarded as bringing good luck. Julius Caesar, when in Spain, was doubly encouraged to see a flock of doves settling in a palm tree he had saved from the feller's axe because the tree itself was a sacred one.

Despite the long association of the dove with peace, tranquillity and love, some superstitions still survive in which it is seen as a messenger of *bad* tidings – an attitude owing something, perhaps, to the dove's long-lived reputation of being a companion to the gods, who presumably knew when disaster was pending. In 1902 300 miners in the Welsh town of Glyncorrig positively refused to go down the mine after a dove had been seen at the pithead. A dove had been similarly spotted before accidents in the Senghenydd and Llanbradach pits.

The high-flying crane, which covers immense distances, wintering under the broiling sun of Central Africa and India but going north in spring, was in ancient times associated with the sun and took from it god-like propensities. Its habit of flying in a V-formation was noted by the Greeks, to whom the triangular shape suggested one of their letters, delta. And since the crane was observed standing on first one leg and then the other, it was assumed to be ever-vigilant and an example to man. Because cranes – and storks – are so regular in migrating, 'so punctual in their comings and goings' Stanley says, 'from the most remote times they have been considered as equipped with reasoning powers'.

During the mating season, cranes perform a curious sort of dance. The movements are so meticulous that they suggest an actual ceremony. It is not surprising that these dances were thought to be a magical ritual, whose meaning and purpose were known only to the birds themselves. As a result, the dance of the cranes was adopted and adapted by human beings – in Crete, for example, and in China – to achieve magical purposes. The Greek island of Delos, where Apollo was born, was famous for its dance of the cranes, in which the movements of the birds were imitated, and a chorus celebrated the escape of Theseus from the labyrinth.

Crane dances in China once produced a tragic by-product. History records that Ho-Lu, ruler of the Yangtze Valley in ancient times, broke a taboo by allowing his wife to share the fish he was eating. She committed suicide, and in order to propitiate the gods an elaborate and macabre ritual was enacted. First, a tomb of immense proportions and superb architecture was built, with sepulchral chamber reached by an underground passage. Magnificent furnishings and hangings were included. Then, in the market-place of the city, the dance of the cranes was enacted. To music and chanting the gaily costumed dancers moved away from the market-place and, on orders from the monarch, the boys and girls followed the crane dancers. In true Pied Piper fashion they followed the dancers into the tomb, at which the passage was closed and sealed, and everyone, dancers and children, buried alive.

14

Animals and Magic

Magic, religion and mythology cannot easily be divided. They are in fact almost invariably related, even though the links of continuity may have been lost in time. Thus one finds birds, beasts, insects and even snakes being worshipped as gods, on other occasions being the medium through which the gods achieve their ends, or the refuge for the soul of a human being, or as a reincarnation. Sometimes animal gods are propitiated and worshipped, literally as gods; at other times they are real animals enjoying the favour and protection of gods. Those who believe that magic was the precursor of religion will find nothing surprising in the fact that animals have always played a significant role in magical ceremonies. Animals themselves, or parts of animals, were presumed to possess magical properties. American Negroes still consider a rabbit's foot a potent lucky charm – and in World War II many an RAF pilot wore a rabbit's foot around his neck when flying on a dangerous mission. A rabbit's foot used to be placed in an actor's first make-up box when starting out on his profession. In a similar instance, Pliny records that one prescription for keeping ghosts at bay was to wear a hyena's tooth, while the blood of a hyena smeared on the doorposts was a sure protection against the machinations of evil spirits.

The involvement of animals in witchcraft is probably a deri-vation of more ancient practices and beliefs. The gods Pan and Silenus, the satyrs and the fauns of ancient mythology, were either goats or goatlike; Ljesche, wood-spirit of northern Europe, was believed to be partly like a goat – especially as to horns, ears and legs, and the Bijagos people in Africa worshipped a goat as a god. It is easy to see why, in due course, a horned god became a central feature in witchcraft ceremonies and, by the enemies of witchcraft, particularly the Church, was assumed to be the Devil.

The same is true of cats. Once, they too were worshipped as gods, yet for hundreds of years, especially in the Middle Ages, when the witchcraft mania flourished, the cat was said to be the witch's 'familiar'. If cattle became ill, the blame would be put upon some old woman of unprepossessing appearance, living alone in a cottage, mumbling to herself and talking to her cat – a habit common to pet-lovers, lonely or otherwise, throughout the world. The innocent creature would bear part of the brunt of the hatred and superstition directed by the cruel and ignorant against the supposed witch. The legend of the Devil borrowing the coat of a black cat whenever he wished to torment a victim was a disaster for black cats, which were often burnt alive with the witch. During religious festivals in France hundreds of cats used to be thrown alive onto a bonfire as a sacrifice (even in those cruel times, King Louis XIII, when he was Dauphin, made an effort to stop the practice); in England the coronation of Queen Elizabeth I was 'celebrated' by the burning of an effigy of the Pope, which had been stuffed with live cats whose frantic struggles caused the effigy to move and writhe realistically when set afire.

Animal worship, which pervaded the ancient world and shows signs of survival in modern times, exemplifies how religion, myth and magic intertwine. The cult of Artemis – Diana to the Romans – was a complicated one. In ancient Greece, she had a number of shrines where she was worshipped variously as patroness of the young and protector of the flocks, and of the chase, as well as moon goddess. The oldest accounts make her the twin sister of Apollo, born with him on the island of Delos. Where Apollo is regarded as sun god, Artemis, embodying the female principle, becomes Selene, or moon goddess. As such she is unmoved by love and vowed to chastity. The Arcadian Artemis is also leader of the virgin nymphs, with whom she goes hunting in the mountains. It is in this role as huntress that she is best known and most frequently represented in paintings and pictures. With bow and arrow, surrounded by hounds and stag, she appears in innumerable works of art – one of the most famous being the Diana in the Paris Louvre.

But Artemis shares with her brother, Apollo, powers over life and death. Her life-enhancing gifts make her worshipped as goddess of procreation. So the virgin goddess – free, lively and fearless – sometimes watches over women in childbirth, taking over from another minor fertility goddess, Ilithya. And when she presides at pre-nuptial festivals the bear becomes her symbol: the young brides-to-be dressed in bearskins dance in her honour to secure a blessing on their union. The bear theme goes back a long way. In her primitive aspect as an agricultural deity, Artemis had a constant companion, Callisto, beloved by Zeus, who turned her into a she-bear to hide her from his wife. Later he placed her among the stars as Arctos, the Bear.

It is quite likely that Artemis and Callisto become confused, and one is tempted to connect them with Artio, the Celtic goddess of the Helvetii, the modern Swiss, whose symbol was also a she-bear. In 1832 a statue of Artio, as bear goddess, was dug up near Berne. Perhaps the little hand-carved wooden bears collected by generations of tourists are a final manifestation of how the ancient fertility cult spread from far-away Greece to Switzerland.

Snakes have enjoyed a mystical reputation for thousands of years. They have been an accessory in magical ceremonies; they have been worshipped as gods and have been a feature of many secret societies. The reasons are not difficult to understand. Firstly, the snake is distinctly a phallic symbol and – as Freud and the psychoanalysts made plain – typifies fecundity and rebirth. Seeming to issue from the underworld, their ability to shed their skins and still live suggested reincarnation.

For most of the Christian world, the snake makes its first momentous appearance in the Book of Genesis, where he tempts the Woman to taste the apple, the fruit symbolizing carnal knowledge. For this wicked act God chases Adam and Eve out of the Garden of Eden and puts everlasting enmity between women and snakes. There exists, however, a slightly different version: in Hebrew mythology, the snake itself seduces Eve, fathering Cain, the fratricide, on her. But in older cults the snake's carnal encounter with the woman gave rise to a fertility cult. Sacred serpents were kept in Egyptian temples to act as the gods' procreative agents. In Greece, snakes were sacred to the god of medicine, Aesculapius. Barren women would lie naked all night in his temple hoping that he would take the form of a snake and impregnate them. The association of snakes with healing is still commemorated in the familiar medical symbol used by doctors to this day – the staff of Aesculapius with a serpent coiled round it. The snake itself as a healer appears in the legend that tells how the blind emperor Theodosius had his sight restored when a serpent laid a precious stone upon his eyes.

The cult of the snake is as ancient as it is widespread. An earth goddess, dating back to 1600-1580 BC, with bare breasts and a snake in each hand, was found in Crete in the Palace of Knossos. It re-appears in many forms in Africa. In West Africa under French colonial rule, fifty snakes were kept in a serpent temple in Dahomey (Benin). So sacred were these pythons that to kill one even outside the temple precincts was punishable by death.

In other parts of Africa, each species of snake was believed to be the reincarnation of members of a particular tribe. That snake-worship was practically world-wide is suggested by the fact that it is found in South America, with the god Quetzalcoatl, as well as in India, where, until the turn of the century, hundreds of thousands of Indians were still worshipping snake-gods (*The Popular Religion and Folklore of Northern India*, W. Crooke, 1896).

In yet another incarnation, the snake turns dragon, for mythologists believe that the many stories of heroes slaying dragons are a relic of the serpent cult, when human beings were probably sacrificed to the snake god. The infant Apollo slaying the serpent Python in its lair on the slopes of Mount Parnassus is an early instance of such tales, for Python is commonly described as a female dragon which the earth had given birth to. In the Middle Ages St George, who slew the dragon, became the archetypal hero. And the story of Siegfried, who bathed in the blood of the dragon he slew and became invincible, shows that medieval dragons kept some of the magical properties attributed to snakes.

15

The Psychic Jungle

'Women and elephants,' wrote 'Saki' (Hector Hugh Munro), 'never forget an injury.'

Saki, who was born in Burma in 1870 and died fighting with the Royal Fusiliers in 1916, had early observed the high intelligence of jungle animals and wrote frequently of them in his novels. We owe to him the assertion that 'an elephant never forgets', and it is true not only of grievances that remain to be punished but of kindly acts that have forged a link between elephants and men.

There is a difference between the unthinking obedience of an animal brainwashed and conditioned to particular reflexes by rigorous and continual training, and the affection, protection and intelligent service rendered by so-called savage animals, to human beings with whom they are *en rapport*.

A touching story of the indestructible devotion of an elephant to his master is related by William Baze, a friend of Bao Dai, Emperor of Cambodia, in whose land and in whose company he studied the elephants' habits at close quarters.

In the last century, his late Majesty Gia Long, one of the makers of modern Indo-China, who died in the early 1880s, had an aged military elephant with silver rings on his tusks, who had been severely wounded in battle. He took to the bush, treating and eventually curing himself with herbs known only to elephants:

On the death of his august master he was inconsolable and retired to the Annamite mountains where he has lived the life of a hermit ever since. Once a year, on the anniversary of his master's death, he comes down from the mountain and makes a solemn pilgrimage to the grave of the deceased Emperor. The disasters of the last ten years or so have in no way diminished this faithful creature's pious devotion to the memory of the Emperor whom he had the honour to serve. It is said that, although his tusks have now shrunk somewhat, the silver bands are still in position.

By the time that was written, the elephant must have been nearing a hundred years of age. Who cannot admire the elephant's memory, and even more his devotion?

Stored up in the remarkable brain of the elephant, and inherent, probably, in its genes, are the accumulated experiences and knowledge of over two million years. Skeletons of elephants have been found dating back to the Pleistocene Period, and they feature in legend, history, carvings and statuary as far back as records go.

Their immense size and strength made it inevitable that man should use them in warfare as a sort of living tank. The Egyptian emperor Thutmose III domesticated elephants for all sorts of purposes – for use in war, for ceremonials and for heavy work such as moving timbers and blocks of stone from the quarries. Alexander the Great used elephants for military purposes. Two hundred years before Christ, Hannibal used elephants in his memorable crossing of the Alps. Thus elephants have fought and lived with men for thousands of years. In ancient China the elephant was held in the highest esteem, and in the royal cemetery at Hsi Pei Kang the skeleton of an elephant was found, buried as part of the emperor's entourage.

A million-year-old elephant, in fossil form, was found in China in the sites of K'e He in southern Shensi Province in 1960. Another, found on the Lan Tien site, fifty miles south-east of Sian, was estimated to be between 500,000 and 600,000 years old.

Except in the protection of their young, or when they are mating, or when the bull elephant is in a state of 'must' (when his temper is uncertain and any one who knows about elephants realizes that he is best left alone) elephants are the gentlest of creatures. One of the most spectacular feats witnessed in circus displays consists of the trainer putting his head beneath the elephant's suspended hoof. The lowering of that immense hoof would mean certain death, but the trainer knows he has nothing to fear. Once an elephant has become accustomed to his master, a rapport is established comparable with that which made the aged Cambodian elephant remember his master's grave half a century afterwards. Without any spoken word, without any specific gesture or signal, the elephant *knows* the disposition of a man towards him. All elephant trainers and hunters are agreed on this; they do not use the word telepathy, but that is what it amounts to.

Commander David Blunt, Cultivation Protector for Tanganyika, once described to his friend James Wentworth Day, a distinguished writer on natural history and wildlife, how a native woman placed her baby in the shade of a tree while she worked. Suddenly from the bush a herd of elephants passed by. They stopped when they reached the baby. 'Two or three of them pulled down the branches from the tree. They covered it carefully with a mantle of foliage, so gently as not to wake it. Then they moved off.' They had done this to keep the flies off the sleeping infant.

The gentleness of elephants towards creatures they could crush at a touch was demonstrated a few years ago, at Paignton Zoo in Devonshire. For some time two elephants, Jumbo and Hosbie, had been upsetting the workmen who were trying to build a brick barrier outside the elephants' pen. Almost as fast as the bricks went into place, the elephants reached over the spiked wall with their trunks and knocked the bricks down.

One of the workmen had a brilliant and effective idea. 'Let's try putting white mice on the wall,' he suggested. 'The elephants won't touch *them*. They won't want to reach with their trunks over the spiked wall, for fear of hurting the mice.'

From that moment the workmen could go ahead with their task. A few white mice were given free run on the flat top of the wall. The elephants noticed the tiny rodents and would not put their trunks over them.

The social behaviour of elephants amongst themselves, although no doubt developed by the need to live together, shows traits of sentiment and gentleness more consistent than those shown by human beings. Whereas distressing examples of child neglect, and even of brutality, are commonplace in Britain, no elephant would desert its young. It finds a safe and quiet place for its *accouchement*, while other female elephants form a protective circle during the lying-in, for tigers are especially partial to the flesh of new-born elephants. Even after birth, the baby elephant is protected on *both* sides wherever he goes – another female moves parallel with the mother. If one of a herd on the move is injured or falls ill, the others will try might and main to get the sick elephant onto its feet again. I remember seeing a film of a scene where an African cow elephant had fallen dead, and the rest of the herd tried for hour after hour to raise her, as though reluctant to accept that she could really be dead, and determined not to leave her alone and defenceless in the jungle. It is as well to remember things like this when we talk so glibly of 'the law of the jungle'. The jungle's laws are often more sensible and humane, in their ultimate working, than some of ours. Wars between members of the same species, such as disgrace human history, are unknown in the animal world.

With children, elephants seems to have a particular affinity, and one of the child's sources of special delight is that such a huge and powerful creature can be so docile and friendly. One of the great draws at the London Zoo in Victorian times was Jumbo, who was visited by no fewer than 150,000 people in a single month. When Jumbo was sold to Barnum, the famous American showman, there was an enormous outcry, and children were heartbroken at his leaving British shores. Even Jumbo himself seemed reluctant to emigrate. It had been intended that he should walk to London docks, a distance of six miles, in chains, but he had other ideas. He knelt down outside the zoo and refused to budge. At last, by a mixture of cajolery and trickery, he was crated and transported – only to be run down and killed by a train at St Thomas, Ontario, while making his way along the railway track to the circus train. It would be mere speculation to wonder if Jumbo knew that his future lay in London and not on tour; but the facts are there – he did not want to go, and when he did, he died sooner than he need have done.

The intelligence of elephants, and their capacity to think things out for themselves, is well described by Lieutenant-Colonel J. H. Williams, who in the Second World War was known throughout Burma and the XIV Army as 'Elephant Bill', the title he gave his book. 'No elephant,' he writes, 'works mechanically, as other animals do, and he never stops learning because he is always thinking.'

Personality is not a human monopoly. Every animal has its own, its unique combination of capacities and reactions. Bees may all look alike to us, but it is improbable that there have ever been two bees *exactly* alike ever since the world began. The leaves that fall in the forest may number millions, yet no two are identical. Just as there are no two sets of fingerprints alike in the world, so the imprints of animals have a like individuality. To take a single example: elephants can be identified by their pads as infallibly as human beings by their fingerprints. As William Baze, who spent forty years in the Indonesian jungle, puts it in *Just Elephants*: 'The footprints of elephants, like those of human beings, are all different. Sometimes the nails are most prominent, sometimes the heel, sometimes the imprint shows a closed foot, sometimes a splayed; everything depends on the way in which the animal walks. These distinct variations make it possible to provide every trained elephant in Indo-China with its own identity card.'

The way in which elephants will take a liking or dislike to somebody, accepting orders cheerfully from one master and remaining inflexible with another, is a reminder that they are *thinking* animals. They may also be telepathic, sensing the attitude of individual human beings to them and reacting accordingly.

The most striking instance of this is the experience of Marie Hennessy, founder of Socelex (Society Against Elephant Exploitation) who lives on the Welsh border, in Monmouthshire. In 1975 she completed an overland tour in support of her cause that took her from London, right across Europe, through Africa and the Middle East, to India, Nepal and back again. For the sake of elephants, whose existence is threatened with extinction by senseless and greedy exploitation, she and her fifteen-year-old son cheerfully faced the hazards of the long journey.

Of the rapport by which elephants know with certainty whether a human being entertains friendly or hostile intentions towards them, she told me:

> To me, elephants are shrouded in a sort of mystique. Their very looks puts one in awe of them; it is as though they know a very old secret that makes them superior in some sort of way. Superior to man.
>
> When I gaze at an elephant, I never cease to be amazed and to wonder at its great size and dignified looks. My reaction to the zoo and circus elephant is always one of love and pity, and also fury that these creations of God have been made to suffer at the hands of man. I feel that as we have set ourselves up to be higher than animals we should be their guardians and protectors, not their tormentors. That is why I hate zoos and other spectacles that have performing and/or captive animals and elephants.

Mrs Hennessy's first encounter with elephants was years ago, when she visited Cardiff Zoo. The zoo's female Asiatic elephant, called Caroline, was then about twelve years old and was owned by George Palmer. Mrs Hennessy had asked to be allowed into the cage but had been told that Caroline did not 'take' to strangers and had knocked a man unconscious when he went in to clean her cage. Within two minutes of talking softly to Caroline, Mrs Hennessy was accepted as a friend, to such an extent that the elephant would answer to the call of her name. On another occasion, at a circus called Rikki del Oro, she encountered a bad-tempered elephant, about seven years old, called Maxi. He had a bad habit of trying to pin people to the wall with his large tusks, but Mrs Hennessy, offered the chance of training him and showing him in the ring, struck up an instant friendship with him.

The 1975 tour enabled Mrs Hennessy to study elephants in their own environment and observe their treatment when in captivity. She visited elephants in zoos and circuses *en route* and observed them wild in the Indian jungles. In Afghanistan she made friends with a seven-year-old elephant whose keeper could not speak a word of English. Even so, she managed to convey to him – and get his agreement to the idea – that she wished to be locked up with the elephant for the night. The elephant and Mrs Hennessy became the firmest of friends (elephants are quick to know who cares for them and do not fear them) and a few days later she gave the elephant his first bath in public. Mrs Hennessy is a true animal-lover: 'Where animals are concerned I am fearless,' she says. 'In fact, I am not afraid of anything.' It is this total lack of fear which animals are able to sense.

A few years ago a lion escaped from the zoo and put the citizens of Rome into a panic, the streets clearing as if by magic. A drunk, however, devoid of fear, went up to the lion, whispered in his ear and stroked his mane, while people who had sought shelter watched incredulously. The drunk was quite unharmed!

Many wild animals are believed to demonstrate the phenomenon of telepathy or thought-transference. Some years ago Colonel Mervin Cowie, Kenya National Parks Director, told the Fauna Preservation Society in London that he had heard of a family of Africans who were believed to be using telepathy to control lions and terrorize villages. There was, he said, 'a certain measure of proof' that a number of Africans and lions were living together in the remote Singida Province. The men almost 'hunted' with the lions and shared their prey. A 'lion-controller' had been gaoled by one village chief after villagers had protested against killings by lions. The man told his captors that, unless he was freed by nightfall, he would get his lions to kill the chief's cattle. The chief refused. Next morning fourteen of his cattle lay dead. 'There seems,' Colonel Cowie suggested, 'to be something, maybe mental telepathy, between the natives and the lions.'

Fierce as lions are, when defending their young or their territory, or on the hunt for food, they can be as docile as cats – to which family they do, of course, belong. Emperor Haile Selassie of Abyssinia kept lions on the loose in his palace at Addis Ababa, to the occasional consternation of foreign visitors, who tried to keep them at a respectful distance. In fact, his lions were never known to attack anybody.

Tablets and inscriptions from the ancient world show that lions were captured and kept as 'pets' thousands of years ago. The ancient Egyptians trained lions and even managed to train the cheetah, the fastest animal on earth, for the purposes of

hunting. The records suggest that there existed a deep understanding of animals, who themselves seemed capable of
close rapport with their masters. The ancient Assyrians were
great animal-keepers – particularly wild animals – and records
suggest that they were rather kinder to them than to human
beings.

A procession in ancient Roman times, in honour of Dionysus,
in the stadium at Alexandria, took all day to pass through, so varied
and numerous were the wild animals included (there were, for
instance, twenty-four chariots each drawn by four elephants). The
procession included twenty-four wild lions. There were no fire-
arms in those days to kill beasts this size should they attack, and
records suggest that the control exercised by keepers could not
have been achieved by arms and firmness alone. Some considerable degree of understanding, some rapport, must certainly have
been established between animal and keeper.

In *Born Free*, by Joy Adamson, first published in Britain in
1960 and, deservedly, many times reprinted, the world was
reminded that wild animals, even lions, can become attached to
human beings. More interesting still, lions can come to accept
a human being as a friend, and not attack him. Considering the
bulk and strength of a lion, and its speed and cunning in bringing
down its prey, one wonders by what process they come to accept
human beings.

Joy Adamson's husband was Senior Game Warden in the
Northern Frontier Province of Kenya a huge territory which
demanded travelling immense distances. One of his duties was
to enforce the Game Laws, preventing poaching and dealing
with dangerous animals. In the course of tracking down a man-
eating lion which had killed a tribesman, he and his companions
were charged by a lioness which rushed out from behind some
rocks. They did not wish to kill her, but there was no retreat for
them and the lion was very close. So the lioness was killed.
To their regret, they found almost immediately that she was
defending her litter – three lion cubs which Mr Adamson took
in charge.

One of them was Elsa, reared from early infancy to three years
old and then released and returned to life in the wild, a story so

extraordinary that, if proof did not exist, it would probably not have been believed.

Such was the friendship and companionship that developed between Elsa and the Adamsons that she would play with them, walk with them and on one occasion even warned them of the nearness of a dangerous snake. Such was the rapport between the lion and Joy Adamson that they even went bathing together, although lions do not usually like water. On another occasion, when the Adamsons' car broke down, she sat patiently inside while a crowd of excited and loudly gesticulating inhabitants gathered around to see if they could help. Elsa made no attempt to attack any of them, sensing, it would seem, that their object was to help her owners. Elsa often accompanied them on safari. She presented no danger to them even when, in a merciful and carefully thought-out transitional training, they taught her to hunt her own food.

Such a transition posed real dangers for the Adamsons. Hitherto Elsa had been fed; now she caught and killed. Would the blood lust extend to humans? It never did. Elsa would go fishing with the Adamsons and carry home the catch. She even learned to understand a little of human language. Once, when Elsa had killed a wart-hog, Joy Adamson tried to indicate that it would be easier for her to guard her kill in the shade by the water, and called to her: '*Maji*, Elsa; *Maji*, Elsa' – *maji* being Swahili for 'water', a word Elsa had often heard. Elsa dragged her pig to the water.

Born Free was one of those rare classics throwing unexpected light on animal-human relationships. Its great appeal is that Elsa the lioness was not made the victim of whimsy and anthropomorphic antics; she was born free and remained free, and duly returned to her own kind. She did not end in the zoo or the circus, but with her own kind.

As C. R. S. Pitman, formerly Game Warden of what was then the Uganda Protectorate, put it, 'Was she an integral part of those she had so long loved and trusted? Many animals are subject to man, but Elsa is not; she was free-born, never subject, and became an equal.' Indeed, Elsa was returned to the wild, where she found a mate. More amazing still, having returned to

the wild, she yet answered the call of Joy Adamson and brought
her cubs for her to see!

Once a team of American sportsmen came to visit the strange
trio and could scarcely believe their eyes as the lioness climbed
a tree, hugged Joy Adamson, played in the river and then joined
the party for tea as though she was a pet cat – and all this after
spending time in the company of wild lions.

Perhaps the story of the Roman slave Androcles who, in the
days of Tiberius, escaped from a cruel master and, having sought
refuge in a cave, removed a thorn from the paw of a lion he
found there, is not so surprising after all. Contemporary accounts
insist that, on being recaptured, he was condemned to death in
the arena but the lion, instead of attacking him, recognized him
as the friend who had helped him in trouble and, to the amazement (and probably disappointment) of the spectators, caressed
him.

A very similar tale is told of one of the Desert Fathers, the
Abbot Gerasimus, who, taking refuge in a cave one day, found
himself sharing it with a lion. The beast had trodden on the
sharp point of a reed and his paw was swollen. Gerasimus soon
removed the thorn, washed the paw and bound it up; then he
sent the lion on its way. But the lion would not leave his
benefactor and followed him back to the monastery, where he
soon made himself useful guarding and protecting the brethren,
their cattle and beasts of burden. When in the course of time
the good Abbot died, the lion was inconsolable and, to the
distress of the brethren, went to lie on Gerasimus' tomb where,
refusing all food, he let himself die of hunger.

Legends of St Jerome, who lived in the Jordan desert at much
the same time, contain the story of a wounded lion which, on
being cured by the saint, became his obedient servant, attached
itself to the monks and was used to shepherd the donkey which
fetched and carried for them.

It is possible that Gerasimus and Jerome became confused by
their apologists, who wrote of their deeds in the Middle Ages,
several centuries after their deaths. But these tales of the saints
and their animals friends, which were immensely popular at the
time, do show that the Church and the faithful accepted that a

special rapport could exist between man and the animal kingdom. Examples of this ancient understanding are multiplied in the life of St Francis of Assisi: one of the most touching perhaps is the story of the humble grasshopper who came to serve the midnight Mass one cold Christmas when the congregation had preferred to stay snug in bed.

The relationship was based on lack of fear. Thus the Dialogues of Sulpicius Severus, which contain the travellers' tales of his friend Postumianus, who had journeyed much in North Africa, record the experience of an old monk, who lived in the desert about twelve miles from the Nile. The good old man stumbled on a lion, the animal withdrew and, we are told, 'sat down modestly a little way away'. The hermit then went up to a palm tree and plucked the fruit from the lower branches. 'He held out his hand, full of dates; and up the creature ran and took them as frankly as any tame animal about the house; and when it had finished eating, it went away.' The author, writing probably in 405, ponders on this as an instance of the valour of the Christian faith.

In modern times it is generally accepted that horses will get restive with a nervous rider. Moving on from domestic to wild animals, Axel Munthe records that he was able to put his hand between the bars of a cage which held a black panther – one of the fiercest and most treacherous of the big cats – and, tickling its tummy, made it roll over. Even bears, it seems, were among Munthe's friends.

To what extent man can befriend the bear is open to doubt. But all agree that both the Polar bear and the brown bear, which was as common in Europe as the wild boar and the wolf before its great forests were largely destroyed, are solitary animals, fiercely protecting their independent way of life. Wolves hunt in packs; bears do not.

Bears can be killers – one of the men on the second Barents expedition which landed in Siberia in 1959 was gripped by a bear which killed him with a bite on the head. But Dr Bernard Grzinek of the Frankfurt Zoological Society, who tells this tale, says that an unprovoked attack by a bear is very rare indeed. He says he has found only one other account of a bear making a fatal attack on a human being – a lone hunter in Greenland who was something of an artist as well and who left his hut to sketch the landscape.

Dr Grzinek tells us that bears are inquisitive – a Dutch explorer, he says, who spent the winter of 1633-4 on Jan Morgen Island had actually to ward off Polar bears who came to investigate his camp. And Dr Grzinek suggests that this may be why the Norwegian Polar explorer Roald Amundsen (1872-1928) was able without much difficulty to have twenty-one Polar bears caught and trained to draw a sledge.

Alex Munthe's experience in Lapland shows the bear under a different aspect. Staying with a family of Laplanders, he went out one morning to explore the tundra with a little girl as sole companion. They walked most of the day, stopping for a picnic meal. Evening found them in a gorge thickly covered with bilberry bushes. There was a breaking of branches and, to Munthe's horror, a large bear loomed over them, his mouth full of fruit. He tried to seize the child and to make an escape – doubtful, indeed, because bears move very fast. But the child escaped Munthe's grasp, and pulling up her jacket to reveal the wide baggy trousers that Lapland women wear, went dancing up to the bear. It looked down at her, then, turning on its tracks, padded off. The little girl explained that she had only been following her mother's advice: no bear will hurt you once he knows you are a woman. In such a belief there may be a faint echo of Finno-Ugric mythology in which the bear was treated as a messenger to the gods. During the 'Bear Festival', the animal was killed and buried and skis, knives and other valuable objects were placed in the tomb. The dead bear was then asked to tell of all the honours men had paid it.

16

Non-Human Psyches

Ask not for whom the bell tolls . . .

Nobody seriously questions the existence of the human psyche. Other words are used to describe it – abstract words whose meanings are imprecise or given different definitions. We speak of a person's soul, of his individuality, his spirit, his mind. Whatever we call it, there is in everyone something unique, something which makes him distinct from every other member of the human race.

The mounting volume of evidence about animals, in all their infinite variety – from birds and fishes to the smallest insect – is that they, too, possess psyches. It is vanity, it is utter absurdity, to ascribe the psyche exclusively to ourselves. My dictionary defines the psyche as 'human soul or spirit; the mind, considered apart from the body'. Those who have studied and observed animals with the necessary time and patience see no reason to deny them a soul, or psyche.

Admittedly, the soul and ESP are two different things. Extra-sensory perception is the operation of special forms of knowledge, the operation of powers which cannot be ascribed to physical causes. But, both the soul and ESP being non-material, it would be reasonable to expect to find the one where we find the other.

We need not assume that, because many examples of corporate living are found among animals, none has its own individuality. Human beings also organize themselves in the most elaborate way, and although in the process, particularly in such autocratic regimes as Communism or Fascism, they subordinate many of their individual tastes, they remain individuals just the same.

Bees and ants live in highly organized societies, in which particular classes are kept rigidly to their role, yet they differ from each other.

Of the psyche, Eugene Marais says, in *The Soul of the White Ant*: 'That which is known as the psyche or soul is something far beyond the reach of our senses. No one has ever seen or smelt, or heard or tasted or felt the psyche, or even a piece of it. There are two ways in which we can come on the track of the psyche. In my most innermost self I become aware of something which is not a tangible part of my physical body. This awareness, of course, is limited to a part of my own psyche. That of my brother is just as far beyond my direct reach as the psyche of the termite . . .'

His special study of the termites (one of a family of insects popularly called 'white ants' which lived in communities and, in tropical countries, build large mounds or nests) brought Marais firmly to the conclusion that they possess awareness and propensities which cannot be classed as physical and which more properly can be described as psychical. He instanced, too, the black 'road-maker' ants found in South Africa. These make footpaths, along which they move in opposite streams from their nest, the out-going file moving in search of food, the other line returning to their nest, each carrying some kind of food such as grass seed, for their food store: 'One kind of "road-maker" ant is master of a wonderful natural secret which even man has not discovered. It knows how to prevent the germination of the seed, even when this is placed in damp ground in the dark . . . the miscroscope can discover not the least flaw in such seed, yet if you pick some of the same seed and place it in exactly the same spot where the ant places his, it germinates within a few hours.' Three thousand years spent in a tomb opened only by chance had failed to kill the seed's fertility. A mere ant could have destroyed it in a split second.

In talking of extra-sensory perception in non-humans, we must admit our lack of knowledge on what precisely the *senses* of these creatures are. Drawing on our knowledge of ourselves, we attempt to find analogies for taste, sight, smell, hearing and so on. Even within these categories, there is an incredible diversity. But only gradually are scientists beginning to probe the other sensibilities, such as the bat's ability to locate the distance of objects by means of its own in-built 'radar'. Smallness is no criterion by which to measure, or speculate upon, the capacities of living things. A silver-fish seems tiny to us; to a red spider, which is the size of a dot, it would seem like a gleaming monster by comparison. And there are living organisms visible only to the miscroscope which are immensely complex.

Considering the intelligence of ants, therefore, the story Lady Dowding once told, of how she dispersed an invasion of silver-fish (a type of insect which often invades damp places) by merely telling them to go away, is not as fantastic as at first it sounds. There is nothing in the story to imply that silver-fish understand English; we cannot be so sure that the *purport* of what was said did not reach them. Lady Dowding is convinced that it did.

The sources of knowledge, often of a highly complex kind, manifested by living creatures has baffled naturalists. Marais mentions how he hatched the eggs of the yellow weaver bird under canaries, for four generations. He wanted to discover whether particular skills, requiring complex knowledge, would vanish if not transmitted by the example of parents. The new birds were forced to lay eggs without first building their charac-teristic nests. Now the weaver bird plaits a wonderful little nest at the extreme tip of a flexible branch, generally over water. Often these nests can be seen at the end of thin, drooping twigs. They are secured there by a special kind of knot which the weaver bird knows how to tie. Furthermore, while the adult birds are seed-eaters, the fledglings are fed on worms.

What would happen, Marais wondered, if, for four genera-tions, these skills were suspended – four generations of fledglings never seeing such a nest made, never being fed with a worm? The answer astounded him. He expected some deviation from normal behaviour, since the young birds had never seen a nest knotted to a branch (or made one) and never tasted a worm. When the time came for nesting, the latest generation found the right setting for their nests, tied the characteristic knot correctly – and straightaway foraged for the right sort of worms for their offspring!

It is easy enough to write off such remarkable things as 'instinct', but what precisely is instinct? Marais called it an inherited memory. Just as human beings possess in their subconscious selves propensities and capacities pre-dating their rise to civilization, so animals and other living creatures possess 'instincts' which are a complete mystery to us and often go back for millions of years.

Robert Ardrey, in *The Territorial Imperative*, asks how the green turtle, which can weigh up to half a ton and whose ancestors go back 200 million years, can swim the immense distances to Ascension Island, halfway between Africa and South America, to lay their eggs on the island beaches. Why should they go all the way from Brazil, a distance of 1,400 miles, to do this? And how can they? The turtles, which must reach this tiny island by open sea, are not borne on their way by currents. Until navigational aids were devised, the island was difficult even for humans to find, yet the turtle, whose head when swimming is held only a few inches above the level of the water and which therefore cannot see the island until it is a few miles offshore, swims unerringly to its destination through hundreds of miles of unknown and storm-tossed sea.

Are the unknown qualities which enable the turtle to do this a matter of instinct or of ESP? Nobody can say. In any case, to ascribe such feats to instinct is to beg the question – like trying to answer a puzzle by propounding yet another puzzle. Merely to write some mystery off as 'instinct' explains nothing. To me it seems likely that, where we know that unexplained capacities exist in a living creature, that same creature may well possess many other qualities of which we are not even aware. In fact, naturalists are encountering new mysteries all the time. Fabre, the French entomologist, spent a lifetime studying insects and even at the age of eighty was still being surprised.

There was also the discovery of Johannes Schmidt, that all the eels in the Western World are hatched in the Sargasso Sea. They were known to make their way down the rivers of Europe to the Baltic or the North Sea or the Atlantic and never come back. Why they went there, and why they never returned, was unknown. Equally mystifying was the appearance of millions of elvers (baby eels), only two or three inches long, which appeared off the coasts and made their way to fresh water. Then Schmidt discovered that the tiny transparent creatures so plentiful in the Sargasso Sea were eel larvae. So at last it was certain that all the eels of Europe, and America too, make their way to the same place to breed and die. Biologists do not know how they can get there from so many different and distant places. In fact, Schmidt's proposition seemed so unlikely that it was at first ridiculed.

The secret world of animals is, very gradually, opening its doors to us. We know a little more than our ancestors about their ESP propensities, although our ancestors had more day-to-day contact with animals and, in many ways, a better understanding of them.

Sadly, much research conducted, ostensibly, as an objective search for knowledge, has an ulterior purpose. Thus, research into the habits of the dolphin, most amiable of man's friends, is being conducted in America, Russia and other countries with an eye to war. The dolphin's attachment to man is to be canalized into channels of destruction; they are taught to recognize the chemical composition of metal plates so that they can lay mines alongside enemy ships.

The infamy of uncontrolled vivisection, which subjects millions of animals to agonizing, degrading and unnatural suffering, continues with the sanction of government departments and the medical profession. Commercial greed means that whales, elephants and seals among others are hunted, exploited or actually annihilated as a species. If there is anything in Carl Gustav Jung's concept of a universal consciousness, the combined outrage of the millions of creatures which have suffered at the hands of man may well combine to haunt us. We are *all* of the same family, though destiny has assigned us to different roles: in our relationships with animals, we should regard them as different, not inferior. The mounting evidence in favour of the belief that animals may, like humans, possess extra-sensory perception should sober us a little; we are not separate, nor immune to what they think and feel.

Writing to his friend Thomas Love Peacock from Ravenna, Shelley described Byron's establishment in Venice. It had turned into a veritable menagerie which Shelley says consisted of 'ten horses, eight enormous dogs, five cats, an eagle, a crow, and a falcon'. Shelley continues, 'I have just met on the grand staircase five peacocks, two guinea-hens, and an Egyptian crane. *I wonder who all these animals were before they were changed into these shapes.*'

Bibliography

Adamson, Joy, *Born Free* (Collins & Harvill Press, 1960)

Alpers, Antony, *Dolphins* (John Murray, 1960)

Angoff, Allan and Barth, editors, *Parapsychology and Anthropology, Proceedings of an International Conference held in London, England, August 29–31, 1973* (Parapsychology Foundation Inc., 1974)

Ardrey, Robert, *The Territorial Imperative* (Collins, 1967)

Atkinson, Eleanor *Greyfriars Bobby* (Puffin Books, 1940)

Attenborough, David, *Life on Earth* (Reader's Digest/Collins, 1970)

Barbanell, Sylvia, *When Your Animal Dies* (Spiritualist Press, 1940)

Barloy, J. J., *Man & Animal* (Gordon Cremonesi Ltd., 1978)

Baze, William, *Just Elephants* (Elek Books, 1955)

Blake, Henry, *Talking with Horses* (Souvenir Press, 1975)

Brodrick, A. Houghton, editor, *Animals in Archaeology* (Barrie and Jenkins Ltd., 1972)

Buffon, Georges, *Histoire naturelle* (1749–67)

Burnford, Sheila, *The Incredible Journey* (Hodder and Stoughton, 1960)

Burton, Maurice, *Animal Senses* (Routledge & Kegan Paul Ltd., 1961)

Burton, Maurice, *The Sixth Sense of Animals* (J. M. Dent & Sons Ltd., 1973)

Cansdale, George, *Animals and Man* (White Lion Publishers, 1953)

Droscher, Vitus B., *Mysterious Senses: An Enquiry into Animal Perception* (Hodder and Stoughton, 1964)

Fox, Dr Michael W., *Understanding Your Dog* (Coward, McMann & Geoghegan Inc. 1972)

Fraser, Allan, *The Bull* (Osprey Publishing Ltd., 1972)

Graven, Jacques, *Non-Human Thought* (Arlington Books, 1968)

Grzimek, Bernhard and Michael, *Serengeti Shall Not Die* (Hamish Hamilton Ltd., 1960)

Kay, June, *Okavango* (Hutchinson & Co. Ltd., 1962)

Lawick–Goodall, Jane van, *In the Shadow of Man* (Collins, 1971)

Macdonald, Julie, *Almost Human, The Baboon: Wild and Tame – In Fact and Legend* (1965)

Maeterlinck, Morris, *The Unknown Guest* (Methuen, 1914)

Marais, Eugene N., *My Friends the Baboons* (Blond & Briggs Ltd., 1975)

Marais, Eugene N., *The Soul of the Ape* (Anthony Blond Ltd., 1969)

Marais, Eugene N., *The Soul of the White Ant* (Jonathan Cape & Anthony Blond, 1971)

McDougall, *An Outline of Psychology* (Methuen, 1923)

O'Donnell, Elliott, *Animal Ghosts* (William Rider & Son Ltd., 1913)

Pain, Nesta, *Grassblade Jungle* (MacGibbon & Kee, 1957)

Pratt, J. Gaither, *Parapsychology* (W. H. Allen, 1964)

Rayner, Judy, editor, *The Horseman's Companion* (Croom Helm Ltd., 1974)

Reynolds, Vernon, *Budongo: A Forest and its Chimpanzees* (Methuen, 1965)

Rhine, J. B., *Extra–Sensory Perception* (Faber and Faber Ltd., 1938)

Richardson, Anthony, *One Man and his Dog* (George G. Harrap & Co. Ltd., 1960)

Riopelle, A. J., editor, *Animal Problem Solving* (Penguin, 1967)

Schul, Bill, *The Psychic Power of Animals* (Coronet Books, 1978)

Seshadri, Balakrishna, *The Twilight of India's Wildlife* (John Baker Publishers Ltd., 1969)

Sparks, John, *The Discovery of Animal Behaviour* (William Collins Son & Co. Ltd., 1982)

Stenuit, Robert, *The Dolphin: Cousin to Man* (J. M. Dent & Sons Ltd., 1968)

Trapman, Captain A. H., *The Dog, Man's Best Friend* (Hutchinson & Co. Ltd., 1929)

Veselovsky, Dr Z., *Are Animals Different?* (Methuen, 1973)

Vesey–Fitzgerald, Brian, *Cats* (Penguin, 1957)

Wardle, Francis, *Zoo Book* (Odhams Press Ltd)

Wells, Byron G., *Animal Heroes* (Macmillan Publishing Co. Inc., 1979)

Wentworth, Lady, *Horses in the Making* (George Allen and Unwin Ltd., 1951)

Westley, Bill, *Chimp on my Shoulder* (E. P. Dutton & Co. Inc., 1950)

Willock, Colin, *Kenzie, the Wild–Goose Man* (Andre Deutsch Ltd., 1962)

Woodhouse, Barbara, *Talking to Animals* (Fontana, 1974)

Index

Abu Simbel, 49–50
Abyssinia, 15, 23, 83–4, 143, 183
Adamson, Joy, 15, 184–6
Addis Ababa, 15, 183
Aesculapius, 175
Africa, 143, 145, 152–3, 175, 179,
    183–6
Agadir, Morocco, 27
Albert Einstein College of Medicine,
    New York, 141
Alexander the Great, 86, 168
Alexander, Charles, 60–1
Amundsen, Roald, 188
ancient world, 23, 65, 83–6, 89, 91,
    132–4, 138, 149, 154–71,
    173–5, 178, 183–4
Androcles, 186
Andronicus, Emperor of
    Constantinople, 85
animal worship, 23, 83–4, 149,
    154–75
ANPSI project, 58–63
apes & monkeys
    baboons, 145–6, 147–53
    chimpanzees, 145–6
    experiments with, 145
    as gods, 149
    intelligence, 152–3
    in mythology, 143–4
    rapport with humans, 21–2

    similarity to humans, 142–6,
        150–3
    trained to help humans, 141–2,
        149
Aphrodite, 168, 170
Apis (Egyptian bull god), 158
Apollo, 160, 168, 173, 175
Arion, 161–2
Aristotle, 132
Artemis, 173–4
Arthur, King, 169
Artio (bear goddess), 174
Ashworth, Frank, 42
Asoka, Emperor, 159
astral projection, 32, 46–8
aura, 33–4
Australia, 14–15

baboons, 145–6, 147–53
Barbanell, Sylvia, 97
Barcelona, 166
Barter, General, 124–5
Bast (Bubastis, Bastet – Egyptian cat
    goddess), 156
Baze, William, 177, 181
Beagle, The (ship), 146–7
'Beaky' (dolphin), 17, 130–2
bear goddesses, 174
bears, 187–8
Beaufoy (ship), 39

Bechterev, V. M., 15, 30, 65–6
Becker, Josef, 45
Belkovitch, Ivan, 136
Benedict, St, 168
Bernerd, Geoffrey, 52
Berlin, 149, 156
Bible, 155, 164, 168, 174
Bigu del Blanco, J., 32–3
birds
  & ESP, 14, 16–17, 22
  as gods, 161–71
  saving humans, 14, 22
Black Cat of Killakee, 93–4
Blake, Henry, 119–20
Blunt, Comm. David, 179
Bodmin Moor, 123
Borrow, George, 102–3
Brahma, 168
Brazil, 133, 147, 169
British Museum, London, 157
Brooke, H. C., 82
Brown, David H., 137
Buddhism, 23, 159, 167
Budge, Sir Wallis, 155
Buffon, Georges, 142–3
bull worship, 158–9
Burroughs, Edgar Rice, 105
Burton, Dr Maurice, 29
Burton Dassett Hill, Warwickshire, 52–3

Cadoret, Dr Remi J., 67
California, 25, 26, 27–8
Callisto, 174
Canada, 33, 56
cats
  domestication of, 91–2
  & earthquakes, 25
  experiments with, 110–11
  friendships with other animals, 75, 103–4, 106
  ghosts of, 92–101
  as gods, 156–7

  killing & persecution of, 92, 94, 173
  'nine lives' of, 107–8
  precognition in, 104–5, 111
  in the past, 89–92, 156–7
  psi-trailing, 15, 104, 105–7, 108–10
  saving humans, 19, 105, 111
'Chacma Jack' (baboon), 152–3
Charvin, Rémy, 147
Cheops, Pharoah, 85–6
chimpanzees, 145–6
China, 25–6, 143–4, 171, 178
Christianity, 169, 174, 186–7 *see also* Bible
Churchill, Winston, 104
Cicero, 161
Civil War, American, 76–7
Civil War, English, 53, 128
Clarke, Mrs M., 107
Clarparede (psychologist), 116–17
'Clever Hans' (horse), 114–16
Connaught Arms, London, 52
Cologne, 167
Cook Strait, New Zealand, 138–9
Cornwall, 17, 75, 77, 123, 130–1, 169
Cowie, Col. Mervin, 183
Crete, 159, 160, 161, 171, 175
crocodiles, 154–6
Cromwell, Oliver, 128
Crookall, Dr Robert, 48
Crossley-Holland, Kevin, 165
crows, 161–2, 168–9

Darrell, Will, 127–8
Darwin, Charles, 142, 146–7
David, St, 169
Dee, River, 74
Delos, 171, 173
Devonport, 75–6
Dickin Medal, 70
Diodorus Siculus, 155

Dog Star, 83
dogs
  & astral projection, 46–8
  attachment to humans, 22, 69–73,
    74, 84–7
  domestication of, 82–3
  & earthquakes, 25, 27, 28
  & ESP, 13, 17–18, 29–32, 34–6,
    37–68, 81–8
  ghosts of, 48–52, 76–7, 124
  as gods, 23, 83–4
  & learning, 65–8
  loyalty to other animals, 73–6
  & precognition, 38–46
  & psi-trailing, 56–63
  reactions to ghosts, 52–5
  & reasoning, 63–8, 73–4
  saving humans, 18–19, 44–6, 69,
    70–2, 74
dolphins
  bottle-nosed, 133
  Delphinus delphis, 133
  Grampus griseus, 138
  befriending man, 17, 130–4
  illness in, 136–7
  intelligence, 134–6
  in mythology, 160–1
  research on, 134–6, 193
  saving humans, 17, 131, 138, 143,
    160–1
doves, 169–70
Dowding, Lady, 48, 191
dragons, 175–6
Duke University, USA, 16, 57, 67,
  110–11
Durham, James, 48–9
Durov, V. L., 30–1, 36, 65

eagle, 164–5
Earthquake Research, Centre for,
  Menlo Park, California, 24
earthquakes, 25–9
Edgehill, Battle of, 53

Edinburgh, 22, 87, 123
eels, 192–3
Egypt, 61–2
Egypt, Ancient, 23, 83, 85–6, 89, 91,
  149, 154–8, 161, 163–4, 170,
  175, 178, 183
Elberfield Horses, 115–18
elephants, 28, 177–83
Eliot, T. S., 91
Elijah, 168
Elizabeth I, Queen, 173
Elsa (lioness), 15, 184–6
Estienne, Charles, 167
Ethiopia, 149 *see also* Abyssinia
Excell, Mrs Anne, 34–5

Fabre, Jean Henri, 20, 192
falcons, 161, 163, 164
Ferrers, Lady Katharine, 123–4
fertility cults, 175
Fisher, Mrs Sylvia, 35–6
Flynn, Rachel, 14
Fodor, Nandor, 66
Fonda, Mrs Claudia, 118
France, 17, 62, 64, 91, 109–10, 173
Francis of Assisi, St, 187
Freiburg, 22
French Revolution, 86–7

geese, 166–8
Geissen, University of, 28, 44, 104
George, St, 175
Gerasimus, Abbot, 186
Germany, 22, 28, 44, 65, 66, 100,
  111, 115–18, 167
ghosts
  animals' reactions to, 22, 52–5,
    96–7, 124
  of animals, 22, 48–52, 76–7,
    92–101, 122–9
Gibbon, T., 125–6
goats, 172
Gough, Charles, 69

Gray, Thomas, 90
Great Plague of London, 92
Greece, Ancient, 84, 86, 132–3, 159,
    160–1, 172, 173–4, 175
'Green', H. L., 99–100
Gregory, St, 169
Grenadier Public House, London, 52
Greyfriars Bobby, 22, 87
Griefenberg, Mrs, 99
Grzinek, Dr Bernard, 187–8
Gumley, F. W., 95
'Gwyllgi' (spectral dog), 124

Haile Selassie, 15, 183
Hall, Dr, 147–8
Hampso, P. V., 97
Hanley (ship), 56–7
Harmer, Sir Sidney, 140
Hartnoll, Mrs, 98
Hawkes, Henry, 69
hawks, 161, 164
Hayes, Robert, 45–6
Haynes, Mrs Renée, 31–2
Heatherleigh Hall, Carlisle, 127
Hebb, D. O., 134
Helenus, Abbot, 155
Hennessy, Marie, 181–3
Henthorne, Mr & Mrs T., 105
Hermetic Order of the Golden
    Dawn, 94
Herne the Hunter, 122, 123
Herodotus, 165
Hicks, Kirsten, 14–15
High Down, Pirton, Herts, 128
Holman, Bob, 130
homing behaviour, *see* psi-trailing
horse whisperers, 120–1
horses
    attachment to humans, 112–13
    as death visitants, 127
    'gentling', 119–21
    as ghosts, 122–9
    psychokinesis, 126–7

& reasoning, 113–18
    seeing ghosts, 124
    telepathic, 16, 113–21
Horus (Egyptian falcon god),
    161–163
Hudson, J. J., 105
Hugh Capet, King of France, 122
Humber, River, 71
hyenas, 172
Hywel Dda ap Cadell (Howell the
    Good), 91

India, 143, 159, 175
insects, 190–1
Isle of Man, 131
Italy, 27
Ivanova, Barbara, 110

Jack the Ripper, 40–1
Japan, 57, 168
Jerome, St, 186
Jobson, Mr, 61–2
Johnson, Dr Samuel, 90, 166
Julius Caesar, 170
Jumbo, 180
Jung, Carl Gustav, 149–50, 193
Juno, 166
Jupiter, 164, 166

Kay, June, 15
Kazhinsky, B. B., 31
Kenya, 184–6
Killakee, Black Cat of, 93–4
Kindermann, Fräulein, 66
Kipling, Mrs Barbara, 52
Kirlian, Semian, 33–4
Kosenko (Japanese goddess), 168
Krall, Karl, 116–17

'Lady' (horse), 118–19
Lake District, 69
Lakhtin, Prof. L. K., 30
Lapland, 188

Lautenschlager, Sergeant, 101
Lee, Sir Henry, 39–40
Lilly, Dr John, 134–6
lions, 183–6
Liverpool, 75, 134–6
Llangollen, 102–3
London, 40–1, 52, 62, 72, 75, 91, 92, 105, 146, 157, 159, 168, 180
Louis XIII, King of France, 173
Lousada family, 19
Louvre, Paris, 154, 159, 174

McAssey, Tom, 93–4
Macauley, Rose, 166
Macdonald, Julie, 152
McDougall, Dr William, 20, 63–4, 81, 118
Mackenzie, Dr William, 66
McMahon, Francis, 44
Maeterlinck, Maurice, 117–18
Magdeburg, 111
magic & animals, 172–6
Mante, Willem, 56–7
Marais, Eugene, 144–6, 150–3, 190, 191–2
Margolis, Richard, 26
Marie Leczinska, Queen of France, 90
Marineland, Florida, 134, 135
Markyate, Herts, 123–4
Marquis, Don, 91
Martinique, 28
Mattingley, Frank, 44
Menes, Pharoah, 155
Menorca, 13
Minogue, Tim, 43
Minotaur, 159
Mithras, cult of, 158–9
Mohammed, 90
Monery, Keith, 17
Monkey (Chinese mythical figure), 143–4
monkeys, *see* apes & monkeys

Mont (Egyptian hawk/bull god), 161
Morocco, 27
Morris, Dr Robert L., 119
Morton, H. V., 166
Muhamed (horse), 116–18
Muller, Max, 66
Mumling, River, 101
Munthe, Axel, 148, 153, 187, 188
Murray, Dr Gilbert, 29

Napoleon, 88, 91, 164–5
National Canine Defence League, 70, 75
Nebti (Egyptian snake goddess), 161
Nekhebet (Egyptian vulture goddess), 161
New York, 141–2
New Zealand, 138–9
Nichols, Beverley, 106
Ningirsu (Assyrian eagle god), 161
Noah, 169
Norris, Kenneth S., 137

O'Connor, Mrs T. P., 41, 73
O'Donnell, Elliott, 50, 98, 126
Odin (Woden), 122, 167, 168
Ofgren, Dr Lars, 133
Oppian, 132
Otis, Dr Karl, 58, 110
Oxenby Manor House, 98–9
Oxwick church, Pembrokeshire, 122

Pachmore, St, 155
Pan, 172
panthers, 187
Panton, Col., 76–7
Paris, 148, 153, 154
Paul the Hermit, St, 168
'Pelorus Jack' (dolphin), 138–40
Penguin, The (ship), 139
Peninsular War, 128–9
phoenix, 165
pigeons, 16

Pleimes, Dr Ute, 28, 44, 104
Pliny the Elder, 132, 143, 160, 167,
    172
Plunkett, Lord, 139
Pompeii, 84–5
Pookas, 122
Pooley, W. T., 75
Pratt, Prof. J. Gaither, 16, 46, 58, 61,
    67
precognition, 21, 24, 38–46, 104–5,
    111
psi-factors, 16, 21, 29, 66
psi-trailing, 15, 38, 56–63, 104,
    105–7, 108–10
psychokinesis, 24, 126–7
Pugh, Mrs Gwen, 77
Pythagoras, 84

Queen's University, Ontario, 33
Quetzalcoatl, 175
Quiller-Couch, Sir Arthur, 124

rabbits, 33
rabbit's foot, 172
ravens, 168–9
Reichenbach, Baron von, 34
Richard II, 123
Rhine, Prof. J. B., 16, 18, 46, 57f,
    106, 108, 118
Rhodes, 168
Rome, 72–3, 183
Rome, Ancient, 23, 65, 84–5, 161–2,
    164, 166–7, 170, 184
Romero-Sierra, Cesar, 33
Rongemo family, 18–19
Ruskin, John, 79

Sackville-West, Vita, 91
Saki (H.H. Munro), 177
Sargasso Sea, 192–3
Schmidt, Johannes, 192–3
seagulls, 14

Sebek (Egyptian god), 154
Sellors, Stella, 77
Set (Egyptian god), 155
Shelley, Percy Bysshe, 193–4
Siegfried, 176
Sierra Leone, 143
Silenus, 172
Simonet, Oscar, 13
Simpson, John, 76–7
Skopje, Yugoslavia, 27
Smalley, Mrs Vivienne, 53–4
snake goddesses, 161, 175
snakes, 174–6
Society for Psychical Research, 16,
    22, 29, 55, 58, 99
    Journal of, 29
South Africa, 144–5, 147–8, 152–3,
    190
Soviet Union, 15–16, 27, 30–1,
    33–4, 65–6, 110, 136
Stanley, Edward, 167, 169
Stead, W. T., 48, 124
Steccoti, Ninda, 27
Storey, Miss P. C., 54–5
Strong, Sue, 141–2
Sudan, 149
Sulpicius Severus, 187
'Swansea Jack' (dog), 71
Sweden, 18–19, 122, 167
Swinburne, Algernon, 89

Tacitus, 165
Talbot Inn, Liverpool, 75
Tashkent, 27
Taylor, Joseph, 73
termites, 190
Theodosius, Emperor, 175
Thoth (Egyptian god), 149
Thutmose III, Pharoah, 178
Tower of London, 168
Trapman, Capt. A. H., 37, 61, 62, 74
Tregeagle, Jan, 123
Triptolemus, 23

Tschiffely, Prof. A. F., 112–13
turtle, 192

Udine, Italy, 27
United States of America
  incidents of psychic behaviour, 14,
    16, 36, 59–61, 108–9, 141–2
  research in, 16, 35, 57, 67,
    110–11, 118–19, 134–6

Valembois, Jean-Marie, 17–18
Vasiliev, Prof. Leonid, 31
Venus, 170
Virginia, University of, 46
Volga (Slavonic hawk god), 161
von Osten, Wilhelm, 115

Wales, 71, 91, 102–3, 122, 124, 169,
  170
Waley, Arthur, 144
Waterberg, South Africa, 145
weaver birds, 191

Weimar, talking dogs of, 66
Weir, Major, 123
Wellington, Duke of, 128–9
Wentworth, Lady, 113
Whaley, Thomas, 93
White, Gilbert, 103
Whittington, Dick, 91
Willard, Dr Mary Joan, 141
'Williams' (*Dogs & Their Ways*),
  64–5, 75, 86
Williams, J. H., 34, 181
witches, 92, 172, 173
Wolf, Prof. Gustav, 114
Wood, G. N., 67
Woodhouse, Barbara, 112
Wordsworth, William, 69–70
World War I, 38, 41–2, 62
worms, 81
Wu Ch'eng-en, 144

Yablokov, Dr, 137
Yeats, W. B., 94
Yugoslavia, 27